PRAISE FOR *THE POWER OF DOING WHAT MATTERS*

"Dr. Skaggs guides us through a method of daily practice with skilled storytelling to focus our thoughts and actions that produce our best life. I think he is right! He has guided me for years." —*Stuart McGill, PhD; author,* Back Mechanic; *chief scientific officer, Backfitpro, Inc.; distinguished professor emeritus, University of Waterloo, Canada*

"Every time I work with Dr. Skaggs, I learn. In the training room and the clinic, he has often helped athletes and patients where others have not. His thoughts and methods have improved my patient care and how I approach my life and health." —*Brian Mahaffey, MD, MSPH; team physician, St. Louis Cardinals; director, Mercy Sports Clinic Medicine, Mercy Center for Performance Medicine*

"This book is wonderful. I am one of CIHP's biggest fans. Their work is priceless." —*Lt. Col. Dan Rooney, fighter pilot; founder, Folds of Honor*

"Dr. Skaggs and his team have made some of the best in the world better. His approach has made me and my coaching better in profound ways. His approach often turns 'have to' into 'want to!'" —*Darren May, PGA Tour coach; head golf coach, Grove XXIII*

"This book is amazing and immediately goes on my most recommended book list. It is a must-read for anyone wanting resilience in life. I can't wait to help tune the senses of my kids." —*Joseph Scribbins, managing director, Koch Industries*

"If you want to take charge of your pain, you owe it to yourself to understand the central message of *The Power of Doing What Matters*." —*Neil Osborne, DC, PhD; associate professor, clinical management, Health Sciences University, Bournemouth, UK*

"I know from my own experience as one of the 'regular folks,' Dr. Skaggs and his CIHP team change lives." —*Robin Feder, executive director emeritus, Central Institute for the Deaf*

"The simple but transformative concepts within this book guided me to quiet the noise and recalibrate my life's compass. A must-read for anyone seeking to find that alignment, or for those who wish to live a life with purpose." —*J.B., special operations soldier, US Army*

"Dr. Skaggs has a special ability to help us explore the gap between what we know and what we do. This book captures his simple and insightful way. For almost a decade, I have urged friends and family to do what matters in this work." —*Kevin Bastien, former CFO, Edward Jones*

"The journey is the reward. Concentrate on and enjoy Dr. Skaggs's recommendations, and the journey will get you to the desired outcome and destination." —*Carl Bouckaert, two-time Olympian; owner, Bouckaert Farms; serial entrepreneur*

The Power of Doing What Matters

Clayton Skaggs

Discover the Mind-Body Resilience in All of Us

The Power of Doing What Matters

CURI^OUS GAP
PUBLISHING

Copyright © 2024 by Clayton Skaggs
All rights reserved.

No part of this book may be reproduced, or stored in a retrieval system, or transmitted in any form or by any means, electronic, mechanical, photocopying, recording, or otherwise, without express written permission of the publisher.

The information and advice contained in this book are based upon the research and the personal and professional experience of the author and is provided for educational and informational purposes only. The information should not replace professional medical advice.

Published by Curious Gap Publishing, St. Louis, MO
www.curiousgaplabs.com/publishing

Edited and designed by Girl Friday Productions
www.girlfridayproductions.com

Cover design: David Fassett
Interior design: Paul Barrett and Rachel Marek
Project management: Sara Addicott
Editorial production: Kylee Hayes
Illustrations on pages 45, 83, 127, and 165 by John Stephen Sirmon Jr.
Image credits: page 15 (ice cubes), Skeleton Icon/Shutterstock; 15 (water droplets), Nadiinko/Shutterstock; 40 (arrow), PRASANTA2580/Shutterstock; 178 (location marker), V.studio/Shutterstock

ISBN (hardcover): 979-8-9912672-2-9
ISBN (paperback): 979-8-9912672-0-5
ISBN (ebook): 979-8-9912672-1-2

Library of Congress Control Number: 2024920491

First edition

For my daughter, her children, and their children.

CONTENTS

INTRODUCTION

The Challenge xv
Questions More than Answers xx
Rocket Science. It Is and It Isn't. xxiii
The Hope xxv

PART I: TO BEGIN

Every Moment Counts 3
A Most Important Word: Self-Efficacy 5
Goldilocks, Luke Skywalker, and a Cowboy 9
    Phase Transition 14
    Boom 17

PART II: SELF-AWARENESS

Sense and Sense Ability 23
Come to Your Senses 25
    Come to Your Senses: Again 27
Violinists, a Granddaughter, and Swimmers 30
    Practice 30
    Difference Makers 32
    Team 34
Mastery Asymptote 37

Olympic Performance 41
Perception. 43

    Training: Sensory and Sensory Motor Awareness Development

Hold On Loosely 47
One-Leg Stance 49
Juggling 50
Sensory Exploration 52

PART III: ATTENTION – FLEXIBILITY AND STABILITY OF FOCUS

The Present 57
Master Peace: Aligned on Purpose 60
    Re-Tired 62
Game. Set. Match. 65
    Love 67
Poise(d) 70
    To Relax 72
    To Recover 74
    To Win 75
It's the Hard That Makes It Great 78
Commitment 80

    Training: Flexibility and Stability of Focus

Two Lists 85
For Words 86
Reading 87
Ordered Mornings 88
Pause Training 89

PART IV: LETTING GO – PHYSICAL AND MENTAL

Know Pain. Know Gain. 93
Go the Distance 96
Breaking You 97
Race of a Lifetime 99
    Joy 100
    Meaning 102
Pre-Will 104
    The Grit 106
    The Gift 108
The Art of Indifference 111
    To Hardship 112
    To Secure Carelessness 115
Hard as a Choice 118
Rest and Creating Space 121
    Perfect Force 124

Training: Letting Go Physically and Mentally

Breathing 129
Do Something Hard—Voluntarily 130
Lift Weights 131
Be Childlike 132

PART V: ACCESSING AND SUSTAINING POSITIVE RESPONSIVENESS

Where You Stand 135
    Swing 139
    Boat 140
Time Is on Our Side 143
Yes, Dear 145
Congruence 148

To the Moon 150
    Kind of Neat 152
Pearls Every Day 156
Keep Eye on Ball 158
Fortunatus 160
Aim High. Woo-hoo! 162

    Training: Accessing and Sustaining Positive Responsiveness

Establish Your Circle 167
Deliberate Leisure 168
Neuromusculoskeletal (NMS) Hygiene 170
Prowess Development 171

NEXT STEPS

Good Things 174

Acknowledgments 179
About the Author 181

"Everything that exists in this life, does so because of two things: something you did or didn't do."

Albert Einstein

INTRODUCTION

THE CHALLENGE

Joe is a good-natured, authentic guy. Right away you can tell he's the kind of guy that makes everyone feel good about themselves. His conversation is filled with kindness. He is forty years old and has a wife and four children whom he clearly loves. He is a business executive with a large company in the US and seems to enjoy his job. He exercises regularly, including lifting weights, practicing judo, and swimming. Joe speaks repeatedly about how he likes to play and do activities with his kids. He seems to have a good knowledge of his diet and is a man of religious faith. He is in front of me today because he has had repeated episodes of moderate to severe back and leg pain that has him considering surgery. He's confused because he feels he's done all the right things, but even after many consultations with physicians and therapists, he's uncertain about what to do about his back.

"I can't do the things I want to do. Nobody seems to have a good answer to help me," Joe says.

After our assessment, typically 4–5 hours for someone like Joe who has traveled from several states away, I recommend that he do the following: a couple of simple daily exercises, eat more, and, importantly, nothing else. I review with him why his back failed and tell him stories about pain and resiliency.

Joe returns in one month and is very excited. He has experienced only one episode of back and leg pain, and the pain was mild and quickly resolved. He also is fascinated that our latest assessments of him show he has gained two pounds of muscle and lost 2 percent body fat. Six months later, he returns and is not only having no low back problems but is also noticing improvements in his shoulder and knee that had also troubled him. He has continued to lose fat and gain muscle. His prescription now includes more advanced exercises and activities.

Joe looks at me curiously and says, "I can't believe this! I am exercising less, eating more, and have lost fat and gained muscle?! And, I don't have pain anymore!"

This is a common scenario that I have experienced over the past two decades. Individuals doing their best to help themselves become more resilient and falling short. High-level athletes and great guys like Joe seeking advice and care from many doctors and therapists and getting limited or no results. Often, clients report poor understanding of what is causing their problem. Almost always, they don't know why they have their pain. Many are trying to put their health and resiliency as a top priority.

It is 5:30 a.m. on a Sunday, and I am listening to a message that was left at 4:30 a.m. It is from the father of one of my clients. Tim, his son, is in a Special Operations unit in the military. The father is also a friend, and his messages are not usually at this time of the morning. The father's tone is different from his usual delivery; it's to the point and concerned.

He says, "Tim is still having considerable pain and is wondering if you have anything else to suggest."

Tim is one day from a two-week long testing for another level of Special Operations for the military. It's what he has been working toward for years. It has become his life purpose. The testing is a very physically and mentally challenging evaluation to see if you are a candidate. If you make it through this stage, then you have an additional six-month qualification evaluation that is more difficult and challenging. You have probably heard about it. It is really hard, and few get chosen. He really wants to do this.

Four days before this call, Tim notified me that he had a flu, had a fever, and had developed a back spasm similar to what he had dealt with in the past. His back spasm had begun after a weightlifting event a few days previously, where he felt a pop in his spine. He was not concerned about the fever or flu, but he knew the physical demand coming his way and wanted to see if I might have suggestions for his back. He sent me some photos as is our usual approach. He had moderate antalgia, meaning he was bent forward and to the side. Antalgia is the body's contracture or stiffening to protect an injured or vulnerable area. He was trying to stand straight but could not. His answers to my questions and his presentation suggested he had injured his back in a specific way that involved the disc and the fracturing of a thin bone of the vertebrae. I suggested a few exercises, offered some advice, and told a story or two. This type of injury usually takes 2–6 weeks to recover from, depending on the individual's fitness and activity restriction.

Tim's father is calling because Tim is at the test site and does not have much access to communication.

His father says, "He says he is still pretty crooked. He wants to do this but wants to know if there is anything he should be concerned about."

I suggest one additional exercise and tell him to watch for 1–2 things and that other than that, he is not going to harm anything that we cannot fix later.

Tim later remarks that the additional exercise seemed to

help. He says he began the physical tests and during the first day gradually began to feel better. After the first day, Tim says, he never thought about his back again. The testing is three weeks long. The final part of the testing is an eighteen-hour hike with a sixty-pound pack. Tim finishes first.

Tim's story is one of the many examples that I've witnessed of how miraculous the human body can be. It is a wonderful story and education about pain and resiliency. The capacity and resiliency of the mind and body are not just for the young and strong. Our stories include all ages, shapes, and sizes. The resiliency we discuss throughout this book is within everyone's reach.

Cindy is calm and peaceful during her initial consultation. She is seventy-eight, a retired teacher, mother, and grandmother. Her middle name could be "caring." She has suffered with chronic low back pain for thirty years, and in the last year the intensity and frequency of the pain has increased. She is not responding to many forms of care or medications. Because she has already had a spinal fusion, there are few additional surgical options that make sense at her age. Her pain is sharp and radiating from her low back into her buttock and down her leg to her calf. Cindy is also a survivor of breast cancer. After examining Cindy, I can immediately tell she has a very high pain tolerance. Areas of tightness and inflammation that would have most patients jumping or strongly expressing pain, she barely responds to. She confirms my observation as she says, "Yes, I have a pretty high pain tolerance. My appendix burst and I didn't do anything for three days." Cindy's X-rays show instability and degeneration that is very concerning. In addition to the fusion of her spine, she also has a significant scoliosis. As I view the X-rays, I am cringing internally. Often after our assessments at the institute, I can tell clients, "The good news is your case makes sense. I think we can help you." After my assessment with Cindy, I have to say, "I am not sure how much we can help you. I do think we can likely improve your weakness, and therefore it is worth a go."

As with many of our clients, my team and I provide Cindy with neuromuscular mobilization, 2–3 home exercises, and tell her to do nothing else. She was previously doing yoga and various stretches for an hour every morning. I tell her to stop all of those. I sprinkle in some stories of pain, resiliency, and recovery.

Cindy returns three weeks later and expresses surprise and excitement as she tells me she no longer has any pain. I ask her if she means her pain has improved or lessened. She says, "No. I don't have any pain."

She says, "I was very skeptical that these simple exercises would help me. But I did what you said, and nothing else. And, after about two weeks, I started to notice I wasn't having much pain. And then none."

On her reexamination, many of her clinical signs and our assessments have improved. From our electrophysiologic testing, she, too, has also gained muscle and lost body fat. She has not changed her diet.

It might seem like Joe, Tim, and Cindy's stories are about the importance of the correct exercise and/or diet for each individual. And, for sure, those were important components of theirs and many of our clients' success. The reason I used their stories to lead this book is that each story represents the amazing power of *doing* precisely what is needed for the individual's condition or situation and nothing else. All were deliberate and unflinching in their pursuit and their belief.

QUESTIONS MORE THAN ANSWERS

I have been blessed to have crossed paths with amazing teachers, mentors, and clients. It's pleasing sometimes when individuals talk about pioneering doctors and therapists in the field of pain and performance medicine and how they have maybe read their books or took their courses. I have been fortunate to train, teach, and sometimes become friends with them. Similarly, many talk about working with a professional athlete or elite performers. My team and I have treated and trained many of the best of the best. I provide this background only to give you certainty that my team and I have knowledge and experience that is unique.

Over these years, individuals repeatedly say to me, "You have helped me when countless doctors and therapists could not. Why don't more doctors and teams do what you do? I wish I would have found you and your team sooner."

I want to help others experience what my team and I have experienced. When it comes to how the body and mind express themselves, I want to help others to see, hear, and feel what I do.

In an effort to expand our ability to assist more people, I, with the help of many others, created the Central Institute for Human Performance (CIHP) in 2003. Our multidisciplinary group has evolved into one of the most recognized places in the world to go when injured or wanting to improve performance.

Our approach emphasizes assessment more than treatment, questions more than answers, and individuals more than science. Our philosophy for recovering from pain and building resiliency to perform at your highest level centers around how a person is responding to stresses over time. Basically, there are three types of stress: physical, chemical, and emotional. They come from many directions: externally and internally. Most everyone agrees these are part of life and that we are going to have peaks and valleys. Some stresses can be reduced by the choices we make. Some are out of our control.

The primary parameter for how you respond to stresses that come your way is essentially your tolerance to them. Your tolerance is your ability or capacity to endure or act on stresses.

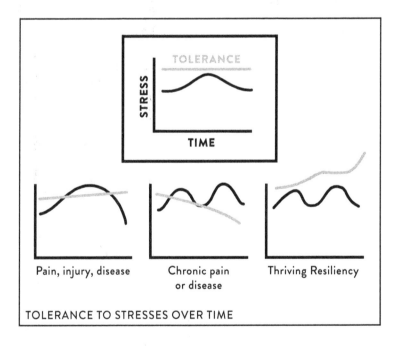

TOLERANCE TO STRESSES OVER TIME

An individual's tolerance to stresses consists of: genetics, traumas, diet/nutrition, exercise/movement, treatment/self-care, and knowledge/experience. The first two, genetics and traumas, are largely out of our control. The other four pillars are in your control and can be more simply categorized as: how you eat, move, care, and think and do. Your development and maintenance of these four pillars is what amounts to your resiliency.

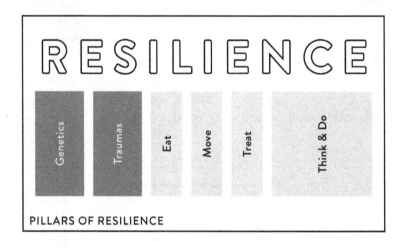

PILLARS OF RESILIENCE

ROCKET SCIENCE.
IT IS AND IT ISN'T.

Our approach through the years has been to help clients and patients improve their resiliency to stresses that have come their way and will come their way.

What we see, and what is supported by scientific study, is that the most predictive and influential factor for preventing pain and disease and improving your tolerance to stresses is the Think and Do pillar. It is the most valuable and potent. It is the hardest to attain. The purpose of this book is to share my knowledge and experience in helping individuals improve this category.

When we review and interpret the experiences and data from our clients, it becomes clear why some clients do amazing. Why they change their life like Joe and Cindy or do something unbelievable like Tim. It is because they *do what matters*. They do exactly what we have identified as essential for them and nothing else.

The field of pain recovery and resiliency building is extremely complicated. Resolving pain and moving people to better resilience and performance in their lives and careers involves interactions and relationships between our psychoneuroimmunologic system, our neuromusculoskeletal system, and our external environment. There is a constant interaction between your brain and nervous system (including your nerves), muscles, and organs, and your external environment.

The estimate is that there are cellular interactions between thirty to forty trillion cells. We humans are not static. We are a vibration of cellular interactions that change, instantaneously, due to moments and events and when we—ourselves or others—observe us. Our bodily function has more factors that are undiscovered than areas of exploration in rockets and/or spacecraft.

Many of the solutions we have experienced that improve individuals are, conversely, simple. Doing less and thinking simpler are often the distinctions that help us resolve individuals' pain, resiliency, and performance needs when others have not.

Therefore, what we currently understand and apply isn't rocket science. It's not trying to take a man to Mars. It's harder.

Aleksandr Solzhenitsyn's Nobel Prize–winning book, *Cancer Ward*, is an insightful, beautifully written story that describes the dynamics of people and care in a hospital cancer ward in 1954 in the Soviet Union. As with many classic writings, the message of hardship and struggle to find meaning and logic in medicine and politics is largely representative today. There is a passage where one of the patients is sharing the news of a possible cure and how peasants in one village don't seem to get cancer. Solzhenitsyn crafts an experience of those mysterious things we maybe don't understand. He describes how at the most desperate times we "catch a glimpse" of what is possible.

He then comments how in our everyday life we don't have time or space for mystery. This certainly rings true today, yet fortunately for us, we frequently get reminded that the road less traveled is the shortest way home. Still speaking of glimpses where mystery reveals its presence, Solzhenitsyn says, "It suddenly flashes at us, 'Don't forget me. I am here.'"

THE HOPE

This is a self-exploration and self-discovery book.

It is a combination of science, stories, and exercises to add to your knowledge and experience. My hope is it will prompt you to rush forward to do things instead of waiting for something to be done to you, or for you.

Many performance and self-help authors repeat that the formula for excellence, happiness, and/or resilience is simple, but hard. That the process is so hard that few will do it. My hope is that this work will be hard, and so simple that many will do it. Therefore, when you think what I am proposing is too simple or too hard, keep going.

The book is structured in five parts. The first part is designed to give you a foundation to support the remaining four parts. Each of the four parts represents the definition and qualifications for resilience: Self-Awareness, Focus, Letting Go, and Sustaining Responsiveness.

There will be questions throughout the book intended for contemplation. These will be mixed with your contemplation of the stories within and the stories that you bring. I want you to *use* this work, not just receive it.

My aim is to improve your self-efficacy. Self-efficacy is your belief in your ability to execute behaviors to sustain performance for a specific performance. For many, self-efficacy is a new word, and its application and importance are layered throughout this book. Directly or indirectly, if you are working on your self-efficacy, you are winning.

Over the past twenty years, my team and I have worked with three former number-one-in-the-world golfers, three former number-one draft picks in major league baseball, three number-one draft picks in the National Football League, two number-one-in-the-world squash players, an MVP of the World Series, a Conn Smythe winner of the Stanley Cup, a winner of the Hart Trophy of the NHL, and a Navy SEAL Medal of Honor recipient (there have been only seven of the latter awarded in history). Of these and many others who were identified as elite performers, Hall of Fame players of many leagues, and the best of the best, one behavior was consistent across most of them: they did not think they were the greatest. Most were adamant rejecters of such praise, placing their attention on doing good things. They all had help and recognized it. In fact, recognizing and helping others was a key factor in their success.

Before you learn how to swim, there can be fear of the water. Water is an unforgiving force in nature, and it's important to respect its danger. Fear, however, can cause tension and rigidity that make it difficult to learn how to swim. The more you learn that you have the capacity to float and move along the water, the less tension and rigidity you have. Before long, you are swimming without even realizing it.

The method I present here is intended to immerse you in the practice of *doing what matters.* Filling your attentional time with known assets for your benefit so you leave minimal to no time for negative or undesirable inputs. When activities and thoughts leading to fear and tension are largely removed, like with swimming, you will be *doing what matters* without even knowing.

This book is designed to intersect deliberate practice and deep work. These are not new words. What is new is combining them in a way that more people can apply them. It is hoped the stories and exercises in this book will help you find simplicity and, ultimately, find your way.

This book can help you transform your mental and physical health. It is the primer for your resiliency. You will be better the moment you begin. To make lasting changes, it may take two years. The more you *do what matters*, the faster it can go.

In the well-known Apple ad of 1997, titled "The Crazy Ones," the final sentence is "Those that are crazy enough to think they can change the world, are the ones that do."

It is likely those that are crazy enough to think they can change the world are the ones that *do what matters*. And, those that *do what matters* are the ones that can change their world too.

You will be advised to do things that are self-evident truths. It is known that they are good for us. Reading, juggling, being childlike, and more. It doesn't matter if you do it well or not. Each moment you participate, you will benefit. One hundred percent.

Legendary running coach and Nike shoe innovator Bill Bowerman would say to his University of Oregon team, "Running, one might say, is an absurd past-time to be exhausting ourselves. But if you can find meaning in the kind of running you have to do to stay on this team, chances are you will be able to find meaning in another absurd past-time: life."

It is my hope that after reading this book and doing the suggested activities, you will find yourself doing what is necessary to be the greatest in your game: that is, the game of life.

PART I

TO BEGIN

"Reality is a cloud of possibility. Not a point."

Amos Tversky

EVERY MOMENT COUNTS

Tom Brady has played in ten Super Bowls. This is five more than the next quarterback, Hall of Famer John Elway. In twenty-three seasons in the NFL, Brady had only one losing season, his last season. He played until he was forty-five years old! The average NFL career is three years. The average age at retirement is twenty-seven.

Is Brady merely lucky? In 2001, Drew Bledsoe was the starting quarterback for the New England Patriots and had just been awarded a then-record $103 million ten-year contract. In the second game of the season, Bledsoe was injured. Not just any injury, the collision ruptured a blood vessel near his heart, and he was bleeding a pint of blood an hour. That day Brady became quarterback and won the game for the Patriots. This perceived big moment then led to a career that has many calling Brady the greatest football quarterback of all time. A GOAT (greatest of all time).

Success stories are often viewed as singular, pivotal big moments. What is less recognized are the millions of smaller or "micro-moments" before and after the big moments.

Had it not been for their successes with millions of small moments, high performers like Brady, Steve Jobs, Neil Armstrong, or Jackie Joyner-Kersee would not likely have been poised and responsive for the big ones. Renowned performance scientist Anders Ericsson qualified the difference between expert performers and average performers as "due to a life-long effort to improve performance within a specific domain."

Moment preparation and achievement, small and large, are fundamental to empower human performance. The same is required to develop expert performance for your health.

One thing you can count on: you will have big moments in the future. Today, 70 percent of Americans report being stressed about their health. There will be moments to manage pain, battle disease, and/or endure surgery. There will also be big moments to help family, friends, and maybe even our culture and society.

Your work and experience in the micro-moments—daily attention to breathing, focused intensity during your split squats, or relentless commitment to a colorful plate—will provide knowledge and actions for achievement in the big moments. In the future, whether it is two, five, or twenty years from now, the deliberate work you have put in will have people saying, "They are amazing to have accomplished that!" "At that age, it is staggering to endure and conquer that." "They were in the right place at the right time." "They must be lucky."

You, in turn, will be saying, "I prepared for this." "I am grateful to have the knowledge and experience for this moment." "I am the GOAT for my health!" "I am the GOAT for my resiliency!"

A MOST IMPORTANT WORD: SELF-EFFICACY

At the crossroads of knowledge and experience is self-efficacy. The broader your knowledge and experience, the greater your self-efficacy. The opposite is also true. Self-efficacy is a cornerstone for human joy and thriving. Underrecognized and poorly understood, self-efficacy has more scientific connections to happiness, pain reduction, and disease prevention than most any other factor.

Self-efficacy was first defined by psychologist Albert Bandura in 1977 as the belief that you have the capacity to execute behaviors toward a specific performance attainment. Self-efficacy can be, for many, an intimidating word. Unpacking the definition can help you understand the value and appreciate the potency of one's self-efficacy. To believe in your capacity is an undertaking. In our time, it is harder than ever.

Your belief, at the end of the day, is dependent on and controlled by you. There is considerable history and complexity competing for it. Most notable and well established is the moment-by-moment information from the digital world. Self-efficacy requires relentlessly managing your attention amid this matrix of influences. Harnessing your belief will require constant wrestling and is a lifelong task. Many people and things are trying to influence your belief and, ultimately, your self-efficacy. That is what makes understanding it and keeping charge of it so valuable.

Consider the average two-year-old. They can be fearless: climbing on furniture, getting into cupboards, and launching into spontaneous runs. They might step off a table! Their *belief* in their capacity is limitless and sometimes hazardous. Then take your average eighty-year-old. They might be afraid with each step, and their belief in their physical ability is extremely limited and sometimes stops all exploration, ultimately ending further discovery. The magic is to *do* things that continue to draw upon our two-year-old mindset for exploration tempered with the wisdom we have learned in our years of discovery.

Capacity in the context of self-efficacy relates to your accumulated psychological and physiological domains and abilities. Are you mentally and physically fit for the task? The understanding of your capacity is likely underappreciated and rarely explored. Knowing your capacity requires repeated and reliable assessment. How well do you move? How well do you think? How strong are you? How inflamed are you? Many of us are resistant to assessment. This must be overcome if you want to improve. Emily Dickinson wrote, "We will never know how high we are / Til we are called to rise." If you don't get assessed by someone who understands where you are trying to go, you will never know how high you are. You will likely not rise, and also not know you need to.

Dr. Jeffrey Rediger is a psychiatrist, Harvard professor, and author of the book *Cured*. In this wonderful book on spontaneous healing, Rediger traveled the world and researched patients who had overcome fatal and devastating diseases: pancreatic cancer, ankylosing spondylitis, lymphoma. He proposed that some of the people healed through nutrition, some through faith healers, some by exercising, and some by changing their environment. He admitted that he fell short of a common variable or magic formula for curing disease and concluded that it is likely different for each person. Yet, what was present in all the cases he described was that each person improved and/or gained self-efficacy.

It is not merely saying "I can do that" or being positive about a situation. It is believing, congruently, that you have the ability to achieve or overcome. Especially when you are not achieving. Most importantly, when you are failing for long periods.

Self-efficacy is not self-confidence. Self-confidence is believing you can do something or overcome something even if you do not have the capacity to do so. We have all known individuals who are self-confident yet do not sustain happiness, health, or success. This key difference between self-confidence and self-efficacy may be the difference maker. Factors covered in the stories and concepts in this book help bridge the gap between self-confidence and self-efficacy: perception, commitment, congruence, and peace, to name a few.

If we want to improve the size and precision of the intersection of our knowledge and experience and our self-efficacy, we might consider the following foundational categories. For knowledge *do*: Read, Listen, Teach. For experience *do*: Move, Something Hard, For Others (see fig).

A prerequisite for becoming more self-efficacious is becoming more selfless. This requires genuine education and learning. When you are working on your self-efficacy, you are not only thinking outside the box, you are simultaneously growing the box too.

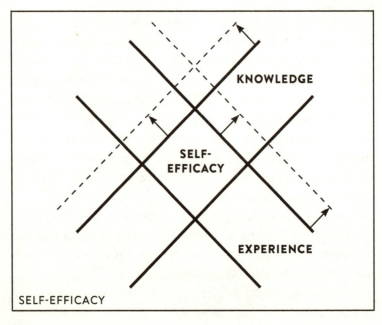

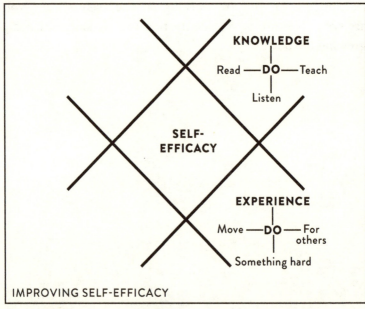

GOLDILOCKS, LUKE SKYWALKER, AND A COWBOY

Bert is a cowboy from New Mexico. He is a real cowboy. He rides, ropes, and runs cattle. He has for over forty years. He is also a master farrier, artist, and gunsmith. It's likely Bert could have been good at many things. As I have gotten to know him, it has become clear he chose these things because he liked them and because they allowed him a simple and meaningful life.

I first met Bert over the phone and then through a virtual consult. A client and friend referred him to me. He was sad to see Bert in the condition he was in. At the time, Bert was suffering with radiating pain down one leg and severe pain in the opposite knee. He had been recommended surgery on both. He was on crutches to get around in his house and was limited to doing few other things. If this guy was using crutches, you knew he was in a lot of pain. He was not only not riding, roping, or doing many of the things he loved, he was having trouble living.

Bert is seventy-eight years old, with white hair and a "Tom Selleck" white mustache. His chiseled facial features and kind eyes make you think of a cowboy in the early westerns. He would be one of the good guys. As we talked in our first meeting, I could tell Bert had a broader than normal understanding of the body and movement, and he asked good questions. I could also tell he was sad. He not only could not do many of the things he wanted to do, but had also been told that his back needed surgery and his knee was bone on bone and it would likely need surgery. With these recommendations, he was given no reassurance he would be able to resume his activities.

As a complicating factor, around the time that these problems of his back and knee developed, he was also diagnosed with a degenerative eye condition, which at the time of our call had left him with minimal vision out of one eye.

Bert sent me his specific photos, called Visual Health Representations (VHR™), which we use at the institute. We will expand on these later. He also sent X-rays and MRI results. After reviewing the materials, I told him during our consult that I thought it would be worth trying some simple exercises and, importantly, not to do anything else. I explained to him where I thought he could improve and how that might help his pain. I also let him know that I thought there was space in his knee joint that could function if given better support and strength. I told him a few stories where others had improved. He seemed encouraged and committed to do as I suggested.

As we have covered, your body is made up of an estimated forty trillion cells. How well your cells regenerate and age is directly linked to health or disease. When you battle a cold, sciatica, or are recovering from surgery, your forty trillion cells are doing their job. They have an unbelievable capacity and ability. From reading poetry to hearing tuning forks to practicing meditation, scientific studies have shown that you can influence your cellular activity and healing.

One of the metaphors to explain the amazing potential of the human body is using the Goldilocks principle. Goldilocks is, of course, the children's story where Goldilocks has her encounter with the three bears, tasting the different porridges and discovering one is too hot, one is too cold, and one is just right. The Goldilocks principle is used across many industries. I first heard it used for pain and behavior education from Lorimer Moseley, a renowned pain education scientist and researcher. His and his colleagues' work and research has been part of the fabric of CIHP methodology for decades.

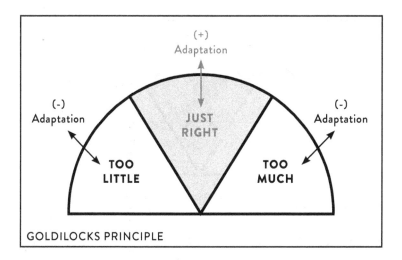

GOLDILOCKS PRINCIPLE

One of my favorite explanations of the Goldilocks principle is its application to a broken bone. When you have a broken bone, it is put in a cast to stabilize the area to heal. If the bone is stabilized just right, the body creates positive adaptations that result in growing new bone. Yes, it grows new bone! After thirty years of working with the human body, I still find these processes in the body amazing!

However, if you put too much pressure on the bone, it will induce negative adaptations. It will not heal. It will not grow new bone. If you put too little pressure on the bone, and it moves too much, it will not heal. It will not grow new bone.

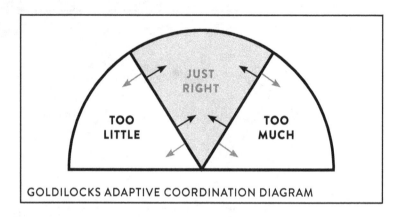

GOLDILOCKS ADAPTIVE COORDINATION DIAGRAM

Fortunately, the window for stabilizing a bone to heal is wide, and it is reasonably easy to hit the target.

The Goldilocks principle is applicable across most if not all psychoneuroimmunologic and neuromusculoskeletal systems. It likely applies to everything from our pain to our joy.

If we come back to Bert, the size or parameter for hitting his "just right" target would have been very small.

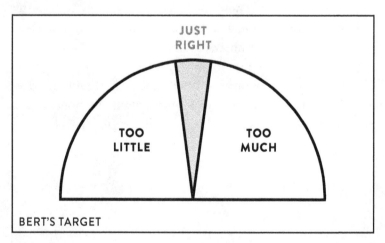

BERT'S TARGET

An important factor to appreciate when recovering and building resiliency is the change that occurs with the influence on each cellular interaction. When you hit the target "just right" over time, the size for the target gets bigger. When you miss the target with too much or too little, the "just right" parameter for the target gets smaller. Knowing your target is important. Knowing if you are hitting the target is critical.

One month after my call with Bert, he reported that he was no longer using his crutches and that his pain in his back and down his leg was significantly improved. He was still having trouble loading his knee, but he was excited in his progress. His VHR™ (fig) was improved. Remember the only thing we had done for this first intervention was provide several simple, targeted exercises such as our breathing exercises, provide reassurance, and, importantly, recommend he do no other exercises or activities. It seemed we were hitting the target.

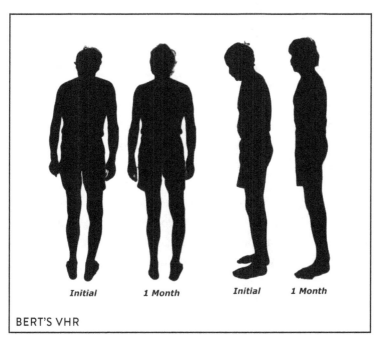

BERT'S VHR

PHASE TRANSITION

Helen Keller, deaf and blind, vividly remarked that on the day she met her coach and teacher, Anne Sullivan, "It was like happy birthday to my soul." She wrote how she felt love and joy through Anne's touch and intentions with wanting her to learn. She stated how she knew at that moment her life would be different and extraordinary. And as most know, it was.

Similarly, I was talking with a cancer survivor, and she related the story of her chemotherapy. She described beginning a series of treatments and having a distinct moment with a nurse. She stated she broke down and became emotional with the nurse. The nurse kindly engaged her and reassured her that she was going to make it through this. She said, "From that moment, I knew I was going to beat this thing." And she did.

And Tim, our military operations client from the introduction, said, "Once I started the examination, I never felt my back again."

Most of us have had moments like these that transformed our lives. Distinct and seemingly instantaneous moments that change us or change what happens for us in a significant and lasting way. The enormity of these experiences is sometimes mysterious and hard to comprehend. One way to describe and potentially define these moments comes from the field of physics and is called a phase transition. A phase transition occurs when two opposing forces spontaneously, suddenly combine to create a new behavior. In his wonderful book, *Loonshots*, Safi Bahcall uses the theory to explain how ideas and businesses fail or succeed. While there are many places to learn about the concept of phase transition, his simple explanation is exceptional.

As Bahcall explains, water molecules are freely moving around and lack stability. As the temperature of water moves toward 32°F, the molecules start bonding and forming tension, and at 32°F, not 33°F, it changes form to ice.

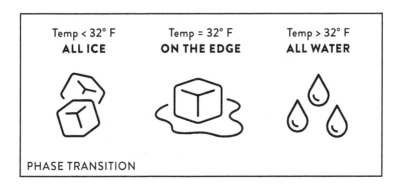

| Temp < 32° F | Temp = 32° F | Temp > 32° F |
| ALL ICE | ON THE EDGE | ALL WATER |

PHASE TRANSITION

There is growing evidence suggesting connections between certain quantum physics principles and responses in the human body. Much of this explains how the mind and body are highly interactive and connected, like how placebo therapies can have such a dramatic effect. Sometimes, this is falsely related as mind over matter. The reality is the mind matters. Norman Doidge's 2007 book, *The Brain That Changes Itself*, helped popularize the idea that brain matter was not fixed. Now it is well known that the brain not only changes itself, but it also likely has the potential to change everything. Deepak Chopra accurately surmises, "placebo" has become an everyday word, but the power of the placebo effect has yet to be harnessed.

Phase transition is a metaphor for understanding the experiences that we have and helping others move toward the experiences they desire.

I remember one of my first experiences of a phase transition early in my practice. I had been practicing only around six years, and I was still under the illusion that what I did or recommended played the biggest role in a patient recovering. I had a patient that was suffering from chronic jaw pain and headaches that were dramatically affecting her life and her family. I had worked with her for nearly two years, coordinating care with her orthodontist and physical therapist. This was a period when temporomandibular joint (TMJ) disorders were a less understood syndrome and, due to their complexity, sometimes led to persistent pain. I had tried on many occasions to help her understand her pain and de-emphasize the uncertainty of the TMJ. I tried to get her to do exercises and understand that there was not anything dangerous related to her TMJ. My message was not landing, and she continued to have pain, limited jaw opening, and headaches.

Then one day she came in and expressed to me, "I don't think my pain and problems are related to my jaw or TMJ."

I was curious to hear how my message had finally connected with her. She said, "I was watching *Oprah* and there was a doctor on the show that said most of these conditions of the jaw are related to the neck and posture and not the jaw."

Within weeks her tightness and limited jaw movement improved, and she no longer had pain or headaches. The guest on *The Oprah Winfrey Show* hit the target and provided the phase transition she needed.

When a phase transition occurs, it seems simple. It is not. In the context of our bodies, it requires a convergence of millions to billions of internal and external cellular communications across the individuals involved and the environment. More than grains of sand on the beach.

That it happens is extraordinary. And it does! The forty trillion cells that got you here can get you where you want to go. Over the years, I have seen case after case and athlete after athlete reach the moment when either a movement, event, or story hits the target, and they experience a phase transition. It's wonderful.

Sensory Awareness is necessary to see, hear, and feel what comes your way or what you need to do.

Focus is necessary to help your thoughts and actions hit the target.

Letting Go is necessary to be poised and indifferent when it matters.

Sustaining Responsiveness is necessary to build your capacity for the future.

You have to believe you can do it. You have to feel you can do it. You have to be capable of doing it.

BOOM

On a microscopic level, there are likely tens of billions of cellular Goldilocks interactions at work for our existence moment by moment. Like grains of sand on a beach. A macroscopic, simpler view would be to consider the four controllable pillars we described in our introduction. Attempting to hit the target in these areas is more feasible and perceivable (see fig). Hitting these macroscopic targets will likely influence the microscopic interactions in many instances.

When you hit the target simultaneously in multiple pillars or strongly in the Think and Act pillar, it can spark a phase transition. Self-efficacy for your resiliency and performance can clear the way for this amazing cellular chemistry to work in your favor.

When you believe you have the capacity to heal or perform, you help move your forty trillion cells in that direction. One of the best ways to create belief is through stories. One of my favorite metaphors for how the brain responds to stories and learning is the "Death Star" scene in the original 1977 *Star Wars* film. David Eagleman, neuroscientist and author, referenced the story and metaphor from the book *The Storytelling Animal* by Jonathan Gottschall during a podcast. You may remember that Luke Skywalker has to shoot a missile into a small portal on this enormous spaceship to destroy

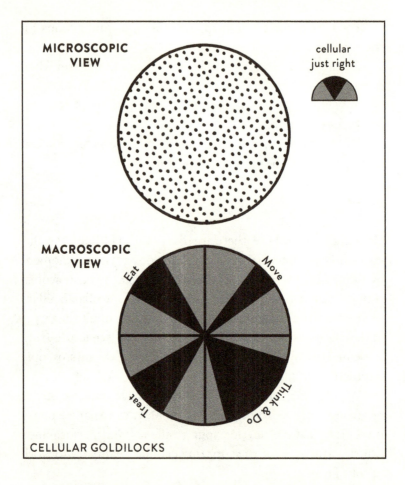

CELLULAR GOLDILOCKS

the ship and save the galaxy. It's a one-in-a-million shot. When Luke's missile goes in the small portal, the reaction creates a spectacular explosion, destroying the planet-sized spaceship. Eagleman proclaimed, "Our brains are wired for stories."

When your brain experiences a story that hits the target, it can create a phase transition, a response in your body, that is as spectacular as the "Death Star" scene. Boom!

Stories are valuable catalysts for our self-efficacy. The right story at the right time can create remarkable, sometimes unbelievable, changes. Sometimes it's like a one-in-a-million shot. The right story can pull other weaknesses forward into a phase transition. Mental and physical preparation and training significantly improve the odds.

Because of his complicated condition, we encouraged Bert to make his way to our institute in St. Louis. He came within a few weeks with the help of his longtime friend. Once on-site, we were able to engage more quality observation, interpretation, manual treatment, and exercise instruction. We continued with pain education and stories of patience and encouragement.

At his one-year follow-up, Bert sent a new VHR™ (see fig). He was riding, roping, and doing many of the things he loves. His right knee, which had been diagnosed as bone on bone, had only a mild bowing, and he had no limp. In our virtual conference, I asked Bert if he had any memory of the pain that had radiated down his leg, when he could not bear weight and had to use crutches to get around his house. He paused, and I could see he was thinking. He said, "Well, I can't remember; it's been so long. I can't remember what it was like." I said, "Perfect."

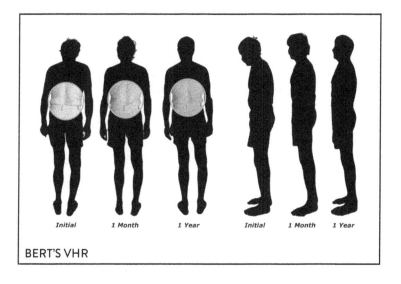

BERT'S VHR

We continue to modify Bert's target for activity and exercise. Bert does his exercises every day. He knows what his target is and when he misses it. He rarely does.

I believe what Bert accomplished is in all of us. The magic starts with the right questions.

The magic can grow and continue with *doing what matters*.

May Bert's force be with you.

PART II

SELF-AWARENESS

"Whoever listens to his body and learns to understand its language holds the key to health."

Mattias Desmet

SENSE AND SENSE ABILITY

The 2019 film *Ford v Ferrari* is full of messages and metaphors. It's based on the true story of the Ford Motor Company deciding to build a Le Mans race car to take on Ferrari. At the time, Ferrari was a leader in this type of race car technology and experience. One of my favorite scenes is when Ken Miles (Christian Bale) is talking with his son about the vision and art of racing. The scene is only one minute and two seconds long. Miles is talking about a car, and there are wonderful parallels for the human body. I encourage you to search and watch now before reading on. Or at least watch later for the full experience and learning.

In the scene, Miles tells his son that you can't push the car for the whole race. He shares his connection with the car as a living thing. He talks about the need to be kind to the car and that sometimes you can hear it groaning. Miles goes on to describe the car as a piece of machinery and how each machine will have its limit. He speaks to the importance of having a *sense* of where that limit is.

Miles then discusses the concept of a "perfect lap": completing the required circuit from start to finish and making every turn at the optimum speed, time, pace, torque, and angle. He asks his son if he can see the perfect lap as they look out at the track. Tentatively, his son says he thinks he can.

Miles follows with "Most people can't. Most people don't even know it's out there."

To push to your limit, or to even know where that limit is, you have to increase your awareness. This starts by developing your sensory awareness, primarily your perception of seeing, feeling, and hearing. There are others, smelling and tasting, but they are secondary. By first focusing on sight, touch, and sound, you can greatly improve your sensory motor awareness, your *sense* and understanding of where you are and how you move. It's why your posture, coordination, and strength are the way they are. You have been building them a certain way for all the years of your life.

For example, the way your hips are currently positioned as you sit and read or the way your head and shoulders are oriented are unique and have been developed by your experiences over the years. How you are breathing, seeing, and hearing are all part of your knowledge and experiences. Whether you know it or not.

Most of us will require a team that understands and celebrates our "perfect laps." Where we should aim, what we should feel, when to push on the gas and when to brake. Cultivating your experience and increasing your sensory motor awareness is the magic that leads to moments of change.

When you relentlessly explore your experience, putting attention to different areas as you move or exercise, you will often find that areas that have had your attention, such as pain or tightness, no longer do.

If you want to push things to the limit and expect your body to hold together, you have to have a *sense* of what it can do. And then, you just might win a race that was thought impossible. For most of us, the most important race is the daily events of life.

PART II: SELF-AWARENESS

COME TO YOUR SENSES

In a major league baseball division championship, one of our clients pitched what some call one of the best playoff games in baseball history. In the deciding fifth game of a five-game series, he was pitching against a Cy Young Award–winning pitcher and friend.

At the time, they were two of the best in the game. Our client was pitching for a team that got in as a wild-card winner, and the other team had won the division. The division-winning team had a formidable offensive lineup and was picked to win the series. Our client went all nine innings in an eventful 1–0 victory. In the locker room, in the stands, and in the media, everyone was talking about how good he had pitched that evening. On the treatment table inside, after the game, our client said to me, "Clayton, I didn't really have my good stuff tonight." He had just pitched and won what is recognized as one of the most exciting and difficult games in baseball history, and yet, he sensed he was not at his best.

How does a pitcher know that? When do they know that? What do they do?

The indication that a pitcher doesn't have their "good stuff" is largely that the ball is not going where it is intended to go. They might say "The ball just wasn't coming out of my hand" or "The ball was not moving" or "I did not feel right on the mound." The success of pitching is centered around keeping the hitter from hitting the ball in a way that would allow them to get on base. The best scenario is getting them to not hit the ball at all, to miss or miscalculate their swing, so that they strike out. To do that, it's crucial to know where the ball is going.

Most pitchers will tell you they know during their warm-up if they're going to have an off night. Sometimes it's not until they are on the mound. The good ones can call on their senses to pull them through. Maybe their feel isn't quite there, so they put attention to their other senses, seeing and hearing, to calculate how to deceive the hitter. During these times when kinesthetic feel is compromised, emotions have to be managed. This is not the time to get more anxious. Not the time to squeeze the ball harder. These imperceptible transitions are held together by grit and courage. Consciously and unconsciously, that is what the best do.

Our senses help guide us throughout our daily activities and during specific performances. Sensory information links to experiences and influences future behavior and/or performance. Your movement is different when you are relaxed, anxious, or angry. The influences from your experiences leap forward whether you know it or not. For example, when you see the ocean or look into your child's eyes, you feel wonder and joy; when you hear a baby laugh or enjoy a favorite song from high school or college, you feel love and certainty; when you smell a cup of coffee or a skunk, you are inspired or repulsed; when you feel the warmth of the sun or the activation of a good exercise, you feel strong and resilient.

Elite athletes like our client typically have a keen awareness of their sensory experience. Referenced earlier, Helen Keller, another high achiever, was deaf and blind at nineteen months of age, following an illness. She graduated from Harvard, wrote fourteen books, and lectured in thirty-five countries. All in the mid-1900s! In the case of someone who is blind and/or deaf, they are forced to practice and gain prowess with their remaining senses. Through deliberate practice, the available senses can become heightened and lead to extraordinary performance. From an elite athlete to a person with a sensory disability, the path for achievement seems the same.

PART II: SELF-AWARENESS

The more you can sense, the more you notice. The more you notice, the more you can control.

If there is a world of sensory information coming your way twenty-four hours a day, then there are likely many ways to practice and improve your sensory awareness and control.

One of the first steps toward developing better awareness is acknowledging the information coming into our senses. Take a moment to look, listen, and feel as many times of the day that you can. These pauses can be formal or informal. This type of exploration can open new experiences that may have you reveling in a sense of where you are or knowing when you need to modify your approach.

COME TO YOUR SENSES: AGAIN

Bill Bradley was and is considered one of the greatest basketball players of all time. He had top achievements at every level. Olympic gold medalist, two-time NBA champion, college and high school player of the year. Bradley is still in the top five of NCAA tournament single-game scorers from when he scored fifty-eight points in one game. What was often recognized was his precision to see plays before others and see and make plays that others would not think possible. In an era that included Oscar Robertson, Jerry West, Bill Russell, and Wilt Chamberlain, Bradley was often recognized as the most gifted player. Bradley performed elegant shots, like the hook shot, that are not included in today's game. He also had a shot he performed underneath the bucket without looking at the bucket. When asked how he could perform such a shot, he said, "You have to have a sense of where you are."

John McPhee wrote a wonderful book on Bradley, borrowing Bradley's phrase: *A Sense of Where You Are*. Sometimes listed among top books to read during your lifetime, McPhee's praise of Bradley's approach to life and basketball speaks to the beauty and precision that deliberate practice and sensory awareness can bring.

McPhee writes of Bradley's prowess that seemed to be present during his early years growing up in Crystal City, Missouri, and how it evolved as he moved on to Princeton and Oxford. Like so many excelling individuals, Bradley seemed to love to practice and did a lot of it. In fact, Bradley was so good at practicing, fans would come early to games to watch him warm up. Importantly, he made it part of his daily activities. He would do vision exercises as he walked and listen to aspects of his play during the game. Bradley's references included feeling the seams of the ball and hearing the dribble of the ball and the swoosh of the net as it goes through. It's as if he couldn't get enough of how wonderful basketball tasted.

Knowledge is sometimes referred to in this manner. The more you know, the more you want to know. Bradley's example suggests that finding something that consumes your senses can lead to doing that something well.

Bradley was smart and curious enough to explore and train his senses. Or did Bradley become smarter because he explored and trained his senses? Most of today's science suggests that it was likely his environment, including the people around him, that encouraged this discipline and practice. Genetics can play a role, but it is smaller. What is certain is that he had extraordinary sensory awareness and was able to do things extremely well and, sometimes, magically.

In any given week, we have clients visiting our institute in St. Louis from destinations like Toronto, New Mexico, New York, Texas, and Kansas. Some to recover from chronic pain and some to improve their strength and health to prevent pain and troubles in the future. After our assessments, they often have the revelation that so many have had: "I had no idea I was standing like that!?" or "I can't believe that I can't do that simple exercise?!"

Then, sometime later when we do our reassessments and they have gained a new sense of where they are, the response is "Wow, I can really see and feel the difference."

Scientific studies and our stories about athletes and patients support the concept of physical and mental abilities being strongly linked. Once thought to be separate parts, mind and body connections are now seen as essential factors in helping pain, disease, and our emotional well-being. What is less recognized and appreciated is that our senses are the information highways that connect them.

If one wants to get stronger; perform better at a sport, at work, or in their family life; or simply be in the best fitness for their purpose, one might consider as first steps: reading, juggling, listening, and asking their health and performance team, "How can I get a better sense of where I am?!"

VIOLINISTS, A GRANDDAUGHTER, AND SWIMMERS

PRACTICE

One of the most fascinating studies on performance for me has always been the West Berlin study on elite violinists carried out by the late Anders Ericsson. His curiosity and publications helped launch the current exploration and understanding of the relationship between science, talent, and performance.

If you were a violinist at the Music Academy of West Berlin, you already qualified as a superior violinist. Ericsson studied what caused the distinctive separation within the elite group of performers. The study required the instructors to rate the violinists as either good, better, or best. Then they gathered information on individual violinists in each group. Ericsson looked at biographical data across large and broad categories: at what age they started playing, how many hours they practiced, how many teachers they had, and how many competitions they had attended. He also asked them to collect personal diaries.

Amid all this data, Ericsson found very little difference between the violinists in each group. Again, to get to this level, most of the students had performed and practiced similarly. Two significant differences came through: *accumulated practice time* and *type of practice*. By age eighteen, the best group had practiced on average 7,410 hours, the better group 5,301 hours, and the good group 3,420 hours. Therefore, the best group was able to sustain and be consistent with their practice longer than the others. More on this later.

The *type of practice* was also significant. The best group practiced alone, by themselves, more than the other groups.

More fascinating yet, all the groups recognized that practicing alone was the most important type of practice. Most of us can relate to the value of this type of quiet, uninterrupted focus. All the students knew this was the most valuable thing to do. Yet only the best did it.

A few years ago, I was visiting my daughter and her family. At the time, there were four of them: my daughter, her husband, a three-year-old girl, and a six-month-old boy. As was common, one day I was conducting my treatment rounds, where I assess and treat them between naps, playing with princesses, and playground activities in the backyard. As I was treating my son-in-law, my granddaughter, while jumping up and down on the adjacent bed, proclaimed, "I am going to do treatment all by myself." She didn't need treatment from Papa. She had seen me do this since she was born. She was really smart. She was a redhead. Did I mention she was three? I simply said, "I admire that. However, I don't think you will find that successful in the long run." She kept jumping.

What the violinists attained and acknowledged about *self-practice* as a differentiator suggests a requirement for knowing what and how to *self-practice*. Coaches, teachers, and peers are often an essential ingredient. These stakeholders along the way likely contribute to maintaining the pace and discipline to accumulate the elite levels of practice. Remember, all groups practiced a lot by any standard.

My granddaughter exemplified wonderful traits of self-reliance and autonomy. What she will learn and we all, if fortunate, will experience, is the value of teachers, coaches, and peers. Self-practice, home exercise, and self-treatment will only be as beneficial as the knowledge and experience that they represent.

> Do you have self-practice strategies to improve your resiliency?

How do you determine them and assess their ongoing value?

DIFFERENCE MAKERS

In the Practice section of this chapter, we reviewed Ericsson's West Berlin academy study on elite violinists and identified that the best violinists had accumulated more practice hours (7,410) than the next best groups (5,301; 3,420). For some perspective, one hour of resistance training, like you might do at your gym or at home, three times a week for fifty-two weeks a year amounts to 156 hours. At this rate, it would require twenty-one years to match the lowest group, and it would take forty-seven years to match the best group! Additionally, the best group practiced on their own more than the other groups. This suggests that simply putting in more hours is not necessarily the formula for greatness or extraordinary outcomes.

Ericsson's and others' studies on performance gained popularity when Malcolm Gladwell's book *Outliers* was published in 2008. Gladwell introduced the "10,000-hour rule" as a measure necessary for someone to achieve mastery or greatness in a field or skill. The suggestion was if you put in ten thousand hours, regardless of talent, you could have elite success.

In a less publicized paper, Daniel Chambliss suggested that focusing on *quantity* was missing the mark when measuring achievement. In his 1989 journal publication, "The Mundanity of Excellence," he identified and described how *qualitative* differences were often the most relevant and, sometimes, the only factor distinguishing great swimmers from novices. Chambliss described how talent or perceived natural ability, as most view it, might not be significant to greatness. In fact, he demonstrated how the misunderstanding of natural talent may lead to many not trying for greatness at all.

Chambliss spent five years as a coach for beginning

swimmers as well as two years researching swimming competitions, from junior national championships to Olympic competition. Uniquely, his research encompassed all levels of swimming competition and performance. Most research on talent and performance is isolated to groups that perform at a high level and after they have already had success. Chambliss's rare view and insightful conclusions could be on a short list of things to read before considering college, an athletic pursuit, or a career. As you will see next, it sheds light on a good deal more than swimming. I like it more every time I read it.

Chambliss brought forth insight that identified how quantitative changes in behavior, increased training time, or increased psyching up or down do not mean you will swim faster or that your arms will move faster or more precisely. Importantly, Chambliss echoed current evidence that simply doing more of the same doesn't result in improving in the sport. He observed that doing more was not, by itself, better. Instead, *what you do* and *how you do it* were the real difference makers.

From his entrenched perch during practices, competitions, and the daily living around the swimming world, Chambliss categorized three areas where *quality* of actions mattered and where it also differed depending on the level of competition. The three areas where qualitative difference was distinct were technique, discipline, and attitude.

The best swimmers moved in the water differently, and even dove into the water differently. They were more likely to be strict with their training, be on time to workouts, watch what they ate, and do warm-ups before meets. They enjoyed 5:30 a.m. practice, long workouts, and hard competitions. The novices visually moved differently, cared less, and would find and express boredom or anxiety ahead of peace and joy.

Importantly, Chambliss suggested that these differences were unique within each level of swimming. The specific qualities that made champions at the country club level, junior championships, regionals, nationals, and the Olympics were all different. He identified that what made the difference in a champion swimmer was often a combination of small things, and these small things were different and distinct at every level. This suggests that as an individual progresses in performance of a sport, age, or, perhaps, health, the small things that are necessary to change, likely change.

Mary T. Meagher, winner of three gold medals at the 1984 Olympics in Los Angeles, changed two primary things during her training for the Olympics. She was on time for every practice, and she executed intense, perfect turns with every lap in the pool, whether it was practice or competition. Most swimmers did not do this. They would turn casually during practices, touching with one or two hands.

Therefore, if a different set of qualities, small details, seems to be needed to differentiate athletes at ascending levels of performance, how do you know the small things to do at each level? Or does it matter which small things you do? Practicing alone, perhaps? And, if this is true, does talent properly describe why someone has achieved success at the highest level? Lastly, how can these performance concepts apply to your resiliency and health?

TEAM

Meagher and several other Olympic gold medalists in Chambliss's study suggest that excellence and high achievement are quite ordinary, while the interest or desire to pursue excellence and purpose might be what is extraordinary. Remember, Meagher chose to make every turn in the pool with precision, and the best violinists chose to practice alone.

Additionally, the current research suggests that individuals are not born with "talent," but that it is learned and attained over time through deliberate effort. Being surrounded by others who are doing the same assists in this level of development.

Chambliss also observed a perception that those who come out on top at every level of competition, especially the elite level, simply "have what it takes." This flawed perception and definition of success as a given talent provides a reason for many to be satisfied with their mediocre performance and/or not pursue a higher level of success. Why work, sacrifice, or dream if the "talent" that leads to excellence and success is something you are either born with or not?

The CIHP team and I have witnessed individuals attaining decreased pain, pain resolution, improved movement, improved energy, improved lab results, improved body composition, and high levels of performance where others cannot. In fact, individuals from across the country, from around the world, and from athletic and nonathletic populations have improved and thrived when others, in the same situation, have not. It is not uncommon that these achievements are accomplished by individuals who do the small, simple things. Sometimes they are prescribed by our team, and sometimes they are discovered through clients' personal experiences. Many times, it requires a combined effort.

Studies also suggest that resilience and good health, like performance, are a multifaceted journey. Recovery and resiliency are products of a confluence of dozens of small things. This is true for everything from cancer to pain. In fact, it is virtually impossible for our healing or health to come down to only one thing. It is ironic and fascinating that our current culture invests trillions of dollars and unfathomable amounts of time trying to identify "the one thing." A single drug or procedure or person to solve our health and pain problems. It is widely recognized, inside and outside the healthcare system, that the healthcare system in the United States is not working.

What remains exciting is all of this suggests that improved health and resilience is achievable for most of us. It is not a matter of some "having it" and others not. As our sign at the institute states, "We believe an individual can choose good health and performance."

If the achievement of excellence in health and performance is mundane, and the actions required are not complicated but rather require simplicity and attention, the bookends of this pursuit might include the following:

1. Like my three-year-old granddaughter, have the grit and determination that fosters self-efficacy.
2. At each level of competition and at different times in our lives, we will need guidance on what to do. This will require the humility to seek, work with, and help others. It is essential to surround yourself with and be part of a team whose purpose is excellence in health and performance.

In fact, Chambliss was later asked what it takes to be an elite swimmer. His answer, supported by his study, was *"Join an elite team."*

PART II: SELF-AWARENESS

MASTERY ASYMPTOTE

Vincent van Gogh is known as one of the greatest painters in history. At the time of his death, he had sold only a single painting and was never recognized by his peers as an extraordinary painter. He faced significant hardship during his life, suffering from depression and delusions. In the last years of his life, he was banished from his village, cut off his own ear, and was committed to a mental asylum. Van Gogh did 900 paintings and made many sketches in a ten-year period. This is a pace of approximately one painting every two to three days. He spent his final year at the asylum in the little town of Saint-Rémy in France, where he produced 130 paintings and some of his most treasured works.

Van Gogh shared in his letters how he hoped someday others could appreciate his vision. He expressed wanting them to feel and see as he did. He also frequently shared how he was hoping for cultural recognition and success. He persisted and was diligent toward mastering his craft despite the significant obstacles. Van Gogh seemed to keep painting for some other reason or purpose.

Van Gogh's journey illustrates an important message that is featured in one of my favorite books and most-used books for coaching. Og Mandino's *The Greatest Salesman in the World* teaches through a wonderful story and a reading exercise. The passage that speaks most specifically to Van Gogh's resilience is in "the scroll marked III." Scroll three speaks of failure and persistence and describes how success and failure are always just around the bend. It reads, "Never will I know how close it lies unless I turn the corner."

Logic and history both support that the road to success

and/or mastering a craft or skill takes a long time. That it will be filled with failures and sometimes long and hard ones. Think Thomas Edison, Abraham Lincoln, Steve Jobs, Tiger Woods, and Vincent Van Gogh. Despite this understanding, and the lessons and books that exclaim that failure is part of the deal, we get challenged, sad, or depressed when failure happens.

The formula that is destined to produce an undesirable outcome is the following: have the expectation that you are going to succeed most of the time or that you will perform something perfectly. Simply reading this formula makes its pursuit seem even more absurd. Everyone knows that this is not a worthwhile approach. Yet, we persist in expecting success with every endeavor and have frustration when missing perfection.

There are rare individuals who seem to sidestep this behavior. One of my favorites is the master boat builder George Pocock. Pocock was relentless in not putting himself in the situation of assuming he was going to succeed most of the time, and he did not pursue perfection. Additionally, when tempted to pursue money or fame, he rejected it. Instead, he stayed strictly aligned with his purpose of becoming a master boat builder. Before his legendary time as part of the University of Washington rowing team that won the Berlin Olympics in 1936, Pocock was an early employee of Boeing. He was awarded stock that became very valuable as the company grew. Pocock was encouraged by friends to cash in. He resisted this urging. Pocock reasoned that this would make him rich, and that could distract him from his purpose: to be the best boat builder in the world. Why would he put that at risk?

Pocock would go on to become one of the most renowned boat builders in the sport of rowing. He built boats for universities and countries all over the world. He helped the sport of rowing grow in the United States and throughout the world.

Like Van Gogh, Pocock wanted more people to experience the beauty and majesty of rowing as he did. In talks across the nation, he expressed how he believed rowing was the finest builder of character of any sport. His pursuit was to grow the sport of rowing to impact more men and women through what happens in the boat. More on Pocock in later chapters.

Daniel Pink has identified this type of craft pursuit as a *mastery asymptote*, and he defines it as "the desire to get better and better at something that matters."

The perspective of this curve can help us keep the highs and lows of developing skill and resiliency moderated. Along the path of mastering your craft—whether that be golf, leading people, or being a parent—there will be successes and failures. Understanding they are just glimpses of time is essential.

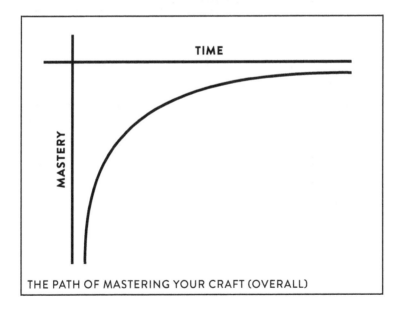

THE PATH OF MASTERING YOUR CRAFT (OVERALL)

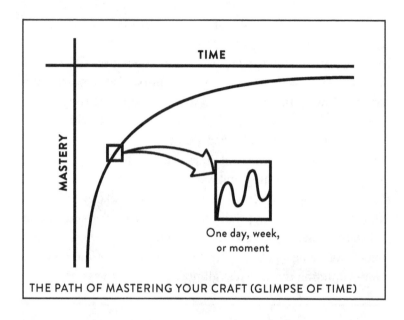

THE PATH OF MASTERING YOUR CRAFT (GLIMPSE OF TIME)

Pocock and Van Gogh seemed to consciously and unconsciously have been capable of keeping their attention and efforts directed toward mastering their craft. They understood, as Pink describes, that perfection or mastery is an infinite pursuit.

We get to work on mastering our craft for the rest of our lives. How cool is that?

OLYMPIC PERFORMANCE

Over a two-week period, I had the opportunity to observe an amazing feat of persistence and performance. The resilience and advancement of skill was extraordinary. After months of preparation, this individual achieved what is still considered to be one of the most incredible human accomplishments. While it is something that many have achieved, no individual has performed it like he did. I had a four-person video team capturing critical moments that I will be using for education with our medical team and with groups for the coming years.

The individual was my eleven-month-old grandson. In those two weeks, he launched his exploration of upright locomotion. He discovered the sensory motor awareness required to move through space and began his pursuit of mastering the valuable activity of verticality. He started walking.

He began with thousands of attempts assisted by couches, tables, and helpful hands. Before he took the first steps, he fell a lot. The falls were not down to the knee or catching himself with his hands. They were abrupt plops from the feet to the buttocks. Boom! Once he was walking, he still fell hundreds of times a day! Again, he was not catching himself with his hands or falling just to the knee. These were full-force drops like slipping on ice or falling from a bike: falls from the feet to the hip, elbow, and sometimes face. Yet he showed stoic indifference akin to Muhammad Ali taking a punch or Roger Federer missing a shot. He often barely recognized that he had fallen. Once, he teetered and fell on a very hard plastic Easter egg that had been glued together to make a musical shaker. Not one of the thin ones. It was thick plastic. The direct fall burst the egg open. He didn't flinch. A few days later I noticed an egg-sized bruise on his bottom.

Keep in mind that with all this failing, there was no instruction or advice on what was going well or what to do better. The only coaching a one-year-old can receive is watching and/or listening to others. There is no YouTube video or Google resource for them.

The grit and resilience to persist is curious and extraordinary.

Consider this fact: babies who are born blind often achieve crawling and walking just outside the norm for development. They learn to walk within similar time frames to sighted babies. Therefore, the likely predictive factors related to this amazing accomplishment—learning to walk upright—are just like many of our successes later in life: purpose and self-efficacy.

When we knowingly want it and we believe we have the ability to do it, we tend to figure out how to get it done.

When you're a toddler, learning to walk allows you to get things you want, when you want. There are big rewards in accomplishing this feat: Parent, food, toys. Also, everyone around you is doing it. You congruently *want* this singular thing more than almost anything. You are pursuing it every waking hour.

Everyone that you love and trust is telling you or conveying to you in some way that you can do it. They believe you can do it. You congruently *believe* you can. If my grandson could talk, he would probably say, with certainty, "I'm all in" or "I've got this."

Perhaps when these two things—purpose and self-efficacy—are aligned, we, too, can be so excited to get to the next step that we pay little attention to our falls.

PART II: SELF-AWARENESS

PERCEPTION

In March 2020, we encouraged our clients to keep their eye on the ball. At those early stages of uncertainty surrounding the pandemic period, the team at CIHP thought taking care of yourself was likely the most important thing you could do.

Then, at the beginning of 2021, we reminded our clients that there were worse epidemics existing in our society. For example, obesity in the US is linked to more chronic illness and deaths than all chronic disease states combined. We shared the history of germ theory, and how Louis Pasteur, the father of bacteriology (the study of germs) is cited by sources to conclude, at the end of his life, that taking care of your "soil," that is, your body and mind, may be the most valuable thing you can do.

Chronic stress is linked to disease. Stress, fear, and anxiety are linked to 30%–50% increases in chronic diseases and increased mortality. In fact, the most impactful factor that puts our cellular regeneration out of balance is chronic stress.

Elizabeth Blackburn, molecular biologist and Nobel Prize winner for her study of telomeres (the measures of our cellular health), has identified that it is not simply stress that causes cellular death and human disease prevalence, but it is also how we perceive stress. In one of her studies, she showed that those who perceived stress as "challenge" stress versus "threat" stress had significantly less cellular imbalance and signs of cellular aging. Perception is everything. In other words, we are going to have stress, but how we perceive it makes all the difference.

Taken all together, it's curious that many of our sources of information over the past few years have encouraged us to "be afraid" (threat stress). It seems prudent to consider and put attention to those sources that encourage us to "be not afraid" (challenge stress).

To build resilience, one might have as a guiding principle to give little to no attention to fear. Be fiercely indifferent to it. Remember, death is inevitable. It is not on your control list, so it should not be on your important list. Instead, give deliberate attention to what makes you come alive. Greet your days with love in your heart. Borrowing some reference from G. K. Chesterton, "storm the castle" for your purpose. Rest your head on your pillow at night.

One of my favorite teaching stories takes place on the African savannas. As herds move across the plains, lions wait in the tall grasses, eager for a chance to prey upon the unsuspecting animals. The oldest and weakest of the lions have lost all their teeth and are no longer capable hunters. They can, however, roar. So, they take their place in the tall grass, across from the younger lions who are the skilled hunters.

As the herds make their way into the area between the old lions and the young ones, the old lions let out a thunderous roar. This sends the terrified herds running in the opposite direction, directly into the pack of young lions waiting to claim their dinner.

Sometimes what seems dangerous, undesirable, or uncomfortable is not. How dangerous, undesirable, or uncomfortable is it, really? And, if it is the difference between life and death, *doing what matters* can be critical.

Identify the challenge, be not afraid, and move in the opposite direction of common instinct. *Do* run to the roar. And nothing else.

TRAINING

SENSORY AND SENSORY MOTOR AWARENESS DEVELOPMENT

"The root of light is heavy. The unmoved is the source for all movement. Thus, the Master travels all day without leaving home."

Lao Tzu

HOLD ON LOOSELY

1. Obtain two identical medium-sized (6–8 ounce) water glasses, ideally made of glass or ceramic. Fill one of the glasses approximately ¼ full and the other ¾ full of water.
2. Hold the glasses in each hand and look straight ahead without looking at the glasses. Move the glasses up and down and take inventory of how well you can tell the difference in the weight of the two glasses. Is it hard or easy to distinguish the difference?
3. Now squeeze the glasses equally and identify if this makes it harder or easier to feel the difference in the glasses.
4. Next, lighten your grip so that you are barely holding on to the glasses. Does this make it harder or easier to feel the difference?

In most individuals, lightening your grip on the glasses allows you to feel the difference in the glasses more easily. The same is true in most physical sports activities: the lighter you hold the racquet, bat, or ball, the more you feel and the better your performance. The same holds true for emotional efforts. The harder you grip or squeeze a situation or thought, the less you will perceive. Learning to lighten your grip on what you see, hear, or feel will increase your experience.

The more you learn through loosening your grip on the glass, the more you will notice differences. As your awareness grows, so will your performance.

Start with large differences in the water in the glass and work toward smaller ones. Put the water glasses somewhere where you will be prompted to do the exercise at least once a day. Do it every day at least once a day for two weeks.

The classic 1980s song "Hold On Loosely" from 38 Special indicates that if we squeeze too tightly, we may lose control.

ONE-LEG STANCE

1. Find a place in your home and/or office where you can have isolated quiet. Next, look for a consistent spot that you can always focus on: perhaps a mark on the wall, a certain mark on a tree outside the window, or a face in a picture or painting. This focused spot needs to be at eye level when you are standing.
2. Next, raise one leg up toward your hip, and put your ankle at the height of your opposite knee without touching the opposite knee. Focus your eyes on the spot, while keeping your standing foot as quiet as possible. Also, be sure you are slightly bending the standing leg—don't lock the knee!
3. Start at 3–5 seconds on each leg, and work up to 10–15 seconds each leg. You need only do each leg 3–5 times.

My valued mentor and friend Professor Vladimir Janda said, "You stand on one leg 85% of the time." As was usual with him, you needn't say anymore.

JUGGLING

Juggling improves focus, relaxation, and coordination, while it's also meditative and grows brain cells, white and gray matter. Learning to juggle is actually very simple, and most anyone can learn. The most crucial skill is mastering the toss. When someone is first learning to juggle, it is standard to see them toss the ball where it would be impossible to catch it. This, of course, makes juggling very difficult.

It's also important to get proficient in catching. If you can toss a ball in the air and catch it comfortably, you might cruise through this part. Stand and simply toss one ball up and catch it. Do this at a height that's easy for you. Watch the ball go to the hand. Sense the ball landing in your hand. Now move to the other hand. Repeat these experiences, adjusting the height of the toss. Next, begin looking ahead while you catch the ball. Continue to toss and catch the ball without looking directly, until you are reasonably confident with this move.

Now you are ready to start with two-ball juggling.

1. First, with just one ball, toss the ball directly in front of your face, from one hand to the other. Get good at tossing it there consistently.
2. Now, start with one ball in each hand. Toss one ball in front of your face, and then scoop your arm to toss the second ball under the first ball.
3. After catching both balls, simply repeat. Repeat until this gets easy and controlled.
4. Now, simply hold two balls in one hand and one ball in the other hand and repeat the toss in front

of your face, toss the second ball under the first, and the third ball under the second. Of course, you will need to catch each ball, but that will be relatively easy after some practice because you are tossing in the same place each time.

Most anyone can learn to juggle, as long as they put in the work and practice. It is important to remember that even poor juggling grows brain cells. Therefore, while you are practicing, rest assured you are getting some benefits!

www.powerofdoingwhatmatters.com/videos

SENSORY EXPLORATION

1. Find a quiet location where you can concentrate, perhaps outside near trees, by a running stream, or simply in your own backyard. The exercise is to focus on one or two of your primary senses while diffusely pairing another. For example, intensely focus on a group of leaves on a tree. Try to identify the different shapes, colors, and movements. At the same time, listen for other sounds you may hear: the wind, noises from leaf blowers, or something else. Continue focusing on the leaves while you gradually become aware of other sounds.
2. Next, mix the awareness of the sounds with a focus on your left foot on the ground. Keep your mind focused on the bottom of your foot while you explore the established sounds and subtleties of any new sounds. Then attempt to switch among all three sensory experiences: the visual on the leaves, the focused attention on your left foot, and diffuse pairing of the different sounds.
3. You can interchange the focused sensory target and diffuse target in many different combinations. The more adept you become at dancing between your senses, the more effective your sensory awareness will become. Later, add smell and taste.

As your practice improves, you can try doing it in any environment. After some time and deliberate practice, your conscious efforts will lead to unconscious performance and discovery. When you first began driving a car, you practiced many conscious efforts to push on the gas and brake or turn the steering wheel at just the right times. Over time these efforts became unconscious, and you were doing most of them without thinking. Imagine heightened sensory awareness becoming so familiar.

Like the violinists in Ericsson's work, if you dedicate the time to practicing these skills alone, you will find it easier to practice around others, and you might find yourself in the "best" group.

PART III

ATTENTION – FLEXIBILITY AND STABILITY OF FOCUS

"The state we think our tissues are in affects the state of our tissues."

Lorimer Moseley

THE PRESENT

Undesirable moments and events are sometimes described as mere "glimpses" of our long journey of life, and keeping them in perspective can be a worthwhile practice. A missed putt, rejected offer, or argument with a loved one. Back stiffness, shoulder pain, or even a pandemic.

Moshe Feldenkrais, a pioneer in movement therapy and behavioral science, is someone whom I have learned from but never met. His work is a resource deeply integrated in *do what matters* philosophy and CIHP methods. One of the most valued principles is his concept of first-person awareness, which he later termed *Awareness Through Movement*. Feldenkrais, a physicist and early developer of martial arts during the Second World War, had some of his foundational discovery through the trials of his injured left knee. After suffering through pain for many years, his inability to walk led him to consider surgery. He was told he had a fifty-fifty chance of recovery and that his knee would always be stiff. He declined. Soon after, he had a fall that acutely injured the opposite knee. He was forced to hop and walk on his left knee, the knee that was recommended for surgery. Feldenkrais discovered that he was able to put weight on the left knee and walk in ways he hadn't before. He was engaging muscles that he had not been using due to pain and behavior.

Feldenkrais relates how he spent "hours on his back" taking inventory of his muscles and movements and, most importantly, the behaviors that were influencing them. By wholly and congruently focusing on his present self and learning new and old ways to move, Feldenkrais recovered his knee problem and never had surgery.

Here he reflects on what he discovered during this rehabilitation: "The present is only a fleeting moment... and what we do with our present selves is the most important thing."

What Feldenkrais seems to be saying is if you want to move forward, it would serve you to master your ability to attain and sustain your present experience. To stay in discovery versus assumptions about the past or future.

Feldenkrais's early insights and training methods are firmly supported by today's science and research. He identified and helped many people by understanding the fluent connection between behavior and movement.

It is said that anxiety is mostly related to thinking about the past and the future.

If we want tomorrow to be different from yesterday—whether subtle or substantial, mind or body—self-awareness and interpretation is essential.

Exploring, discovering, and living in the present grows and expands our present experience. Increasing our present knowledge and experience by *doing what matters* increases our times of certainty and opportunities for the challenges of uncertainties.

Anyone, any place, and/or anything that helps us identify and improve the present is of great value and is truly a gift.

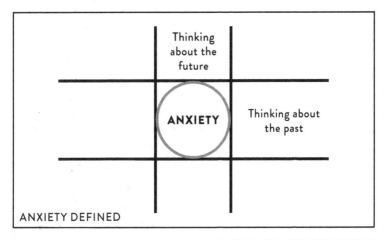
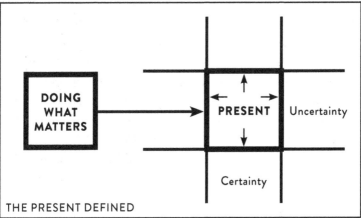
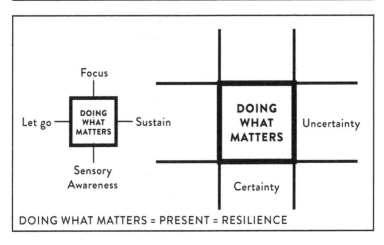

MASTER PEACE: ALIGNED ON PURPOSE

On September 23, 2022, Roger Federer played the final professional match of his career. Many refer to him as the greatest to ever play the game of tennis. On this night, in a packed arena in London, he fought back tears to express his gratitude. He was reluctant to come to the microphone, partly because he was so emotional, and partly because he did not want the night to be about him. This was the persona he carried throughout his career. A career where millions of tennis fans, non-tennis fans, and tennis professionals who played against him marveled at the beauty of his movement and the effortless way he played the game. In a game where the individual player is at the center of attention, Federer seemed to deflect the admiration. He congruently imparted caring less about the results and more about the art. Whether intentional or not, it made you like him and his play, beautiful as it was, even more.

Former professional tennis champion Andy Roddick, who lost to Federer in three Wimbledon finals, shared curious and admiring views of Federer. He would comment that he didn't feel Federer sweat or strained during the match, that he just looked different.

Of Federer's play in the 2003 Wimbledon final, Mary Carillo, former tennis professional and forty-year TV analyst, commented, "This is some of the prettiest tennis I have ever seen."

Writer David Foster Wallace called Federer's play a "religious experience" and wrote a 2006 *New York Times* article of the same title.

There are many aspects and qualities to admire in Federer's

performance. The most valued, the one I love talking about, was his perceived indifference to outcomes. Whether he hit one of his extraordinary shots or made a horrible shot, his facial expression didn't seem to change. No reaction, simply responding, calibrating, as if he were thinking, "Huh, well, here we go to the next point."

In his book *The Master*, Christopher Clarey also identified Federer's lack of facial expression and described how he could keep his eye on the ball and racquet contact point longer than any player he had ever seen.

This responsiveness versus reaction, poise versus anxiety, and fascination versus frustration permeated and flowed through his existence. On court, in interviews, and just walking around.

It was not always this way. Early in his career, Federer was very reactive and expressive when things did not go his way. Shouting, throwing his racquet. After recognizing this, he became what some called "too calm," lacking in energy or fight in his game.

It appears he found a balance between these extremes right after the death of his former coach and friend Peter Carter. It was the first loss of this kind for Federer, as Carter was the first and most influential of his coaches. Those close to Federer have remarked that this was a watershed moment: there was a visual change in him, a maturation. With attention on honoring his former coach, he was now on a mission. He would say it was a change that took more like two years. He was aware of the need for change and when it occurred.

After his first Wimbledon win in 2003, Federer acknowledged his alignment with honoring his former coach and friend. Carter had encouraged Federer to be the best. What he seemed to indicate was not necessarily the most talented player, but the best in other ways.

Being the best is more than winning and more than hitting

good shots. It is a purpose bigger than playing a game. Federer related, "After Carter's death I really started to work hard."

As he talked during the interview, he frequently wiped away tears with his hands and his forearm, and several times had to gain his composure before speaking. Amid his sincere comments about his family, teammates, friends, and the game of tennis, one of the comments that stands out is "It wasn't supposed to happen this way." Maybe Federer didn't pursue tennis thinking he was going to be the greatest to ever play the game. He seemed to merely *do* what he felt was necessary. It turns out that what was necessary mattered and was filled with activities and thinking that led to behaviors for becoming one of the greatest to ever play the game of tennis. For these reasons, he is one of *the best* to ever play any game.

Through hard work and aligning with a purpose greater than himself, Federer found peace in his game and life.

How many of your shots, games, and/or matches are aligned with your purpose? Is your purpose one that can provide similar peace?

RE-TIRED

In a 2019 interview, when asked about retirement, Federer shared how they were not talking about it, because the more they talked or thought about it, the closer it became. He spoke about his family and friends and how if he was still having fun, that was all that mattered at the moment. Federer seemed to indicate that he wasn't sure when he would retire and that his family and especially his wife were OK with that. I think this is important. When your circle, especially your closest circle such as your spouse or immediate family, is aligned, it makes a difference. When life is uncertain, that support is a game changer. He finished with "As long as the stars align, I'll keep playing." Once again Federer appeared to be deliberately aligning on purpose.

In another article two years earlier, Federer said he didn't think everything had to have a fairy-tale ending. This was after Usain Bolt ran the last race of his career and came in third. This is another example of how Federer seemed to have a mastery perspective that went far beyond a tennis match, tournament, or even career.

At the time of these interviews, Federer was in his late thirties. He was not supposed to be playing at the level he was playing. No player had won Grand Slam tennis tournaments at his age, ever. His twenty-year career was a picturesque parabolic curve, going from unbeatable to unbeatable. Of course, there were certainly times when he was not unbeatable and when he was not winning.

Some of the most poignant stories about Federer are from his losses. For the longest time, he seemed unable to win against Rafael Nadal. Yet during those challenging times, sports commentators would say it was some of the best play from Federer that they had ever seen. After the losses, Federer would consistently reply, "I think I am going to be all right," while consistently praising the work of his team. And, importantly, praising the play of his opponent.

One of my favorite descriptions of Federer is from Hall of Fame tennis professional and coach Mats Wilander. He talks about watching Federer between the points and during practice. How he engages the ball kids, fiddles with the ball and racquet, or tries some silly shot. Wilander claims Federer's behavior in this way is unique. Wilander observed, "He seems to enjoy the feeling of having the ball on his strings."

This eloquently describes Federer's embrace of the experience. He seemed to revel in the sense of where he was.

When do you revel in the sense of where you are? Is it aligned with your purpose and on your "important" and/or "control" list? Is there something where you enjoy having the ball on the strings?

Federer "re-tired" throughout his career. While he is known to have taken good care of his body, he restored and replenished the treads of his thinking and purpose most of all. He may have re-tired each match or even moment by moment. His joy and curiosity were apparent. His unique style of poised wondering and perspective that was aligned on purpose is worth practicing. Be like Fed.

GAME. SET. MATCH.

Throughout his career, Andre Agassi has stated he has always hated tennis. Relentlessly pushed by his father to hone his skills for the game, he could serve a tennis ball on a full court at age two. Agassi's father instilled a fighter's determination in little Andre, which fostered an unusual level of intensity in the prodigy. This intensity, possibly combined with resentment, could be seen on Agassi's face in most of his swings. Unlike Federer, his expression was not that of calm and poise, but of ferocity and anguish. For every forehand or backhand, it looked like Agassi was doing the final rep of pull-ups, finishing a run, or trying to get the lid off a very stubborn jar. Yet like Federer, he was one of the greatest to play the game.

His father was a two-time Olympic boxer for Iran. In his acclaimed autobiography, *Open*, Agassi says, "My dad yelled everything." He relates how his dad trained him with an automatic tennis ball machine, which Agassi named "the dragon." Agassi's dad would encourage Agassi to hit the ball harder than the dragon. The dragon could send the tennis balls at 110 miles an hour.

Agassi's father would purposely look for ways to exhibit his son's talents. Or maybe he was also building Agassi's will, his ability to endure difficult situations. Clearly, he was forcing him to do hard things. Agassi's father once bet Hall of Fame football player Jim Brown that Agassi could beat him in a tennis match. The bet was $10,000. Agassi was nine years old. The tennis pro at the club tried to encourage Jim Brown not to do it. The bet was negotiated to a smaller amount. Young Agassi won.

Agassi related in an interview that his dad's philosophy was that hitting twenty-five hundred tennis balls a day meant hitting around a million a year, and nobody else would do that. His father used some of their life savings to enroll Agassi at the Nick Bollettieri Tennis Academy in Florida. At age thirteen, Agassi was already dominating other players. Despite his success, he hated it there.

Agassi turned professional at age sixteen and began to build his reputation as a talented player. Like most of his career, the early part was full of ups and downs and near misses. His off-court life was a similar reflection. Good relationships, not-so-good relationships, partying, drugs, and rebellion.

In 1992 he broke through with a Grand Slam win at Wimbledon. Again from his autobiography, he said after winning Wimbledon, "Winning changes nothing." He still hated the game.

The other day I was consulting with a young man who has had pain in his back and leg for nearly two years. He had been working with our team for about six months. We reviewed his current symptoms and findings from our assessments. He told us that he was having only minimal pain now and that he had had two periods where he'd had no pain for nearly two-week stretches. I reviewed how all his examination findings, including his movement, strength, and VHR™, were improved. I said, "All of this shows you are better." He was winning. Surprisingly, he was very upset. This young and intelligent man was crying. He was discouraged as he hated that he still could not play sports and was still having some pain. I wanted to jump up and down and say, "Man, you are winning!" But it was clear that winning meant nothing. We needed to change his perspective and get aligned with his purpose.

Like Agassi, and many of us, our client's perspective was limiting his ability to see all the desirable, good things that were happening. If you allow your perspective to remain focused on you, you may continue to think you are losing no matter how much you win.

Agassi won eight Grand Slam championships and was ranked number one in the world three different times in a career that spanned twenty years. For most of that time, he says he continued to hate the game of tennis. Fortunately, along the way, he found a new perspective and meaning in his ability to play tennis. He has said, "At twenty-seven, I decided to look for meaningful things in my life." There were significant people and moments that helped him get his life set.

LOVE

"Game, set, match" is the phrase used when the participant is victorious. Tennis can be a long game. In the context of scoring in the game of tennis, "love" means nothing. Sometimes it takes a while to know where we stand.

One of my favorite stories in the book *The Obstacle Is the Way* by Ryan Holiday is about Thomas Edison finding his electrical factory burning to the ground. The chapter for the story is titled "Love Everything That Happens: *Amor Fati*." Edison sees his electrical factory fully ablaze and tells his son to run and get his mother and all her friends. "They'll never see a fire like this again!" Instead of getting angry, Edison was fascinated by the experience. He rebuilt the factory in less than a year, and within that year increased his revenue by 100 million in today's dollars.

In Og Mandino's popular book *The Greatest Salesman in the World*, referenced earlier, he uses scrolls of short phrases as a tool for repetitive learning. Scroll two focuses on love and reads, "Greet this day with love in your heart." The scroll has a remarkable cadence and continues with valuable messages about greeting most things with love. Toward the end it suggests letting all hate from your veins and filling your time with love.

Agassi frequently spoke of his love-hate relationship with tennis. There were times that suggested love was at the center.

In the beginning, Agassi's dad tried to put him in the best situations to win. Like coordinating for him to hit balls with Björn Borg when he was eight years old. It is apparent that love was there. In his many interviews, Agassi says many people contributed to his success and his finding meaning in tennis. Here are three that seemed to play big parts and might provide some insights for us.

Gil Reyes was Agassi's performance coach for twenty years. Agassi has said that he was one of the individuals who saved his life. While Agassi detested the training and liquid concoctions that Reyes would prescribe, he credits Reyes with making him stronger and resilient when he needed it most. Agassi also credits him with a love and commitment that changed his perspective.

Brad Gilbert came along and helped trigger Agassi's second elite period of play. Gilbert, a former player, was the coach that seemed to be an ingredient in the middle of Agassi's understanding toward finding balance in his approach to the game. These experiences coincided with or maybe resulted in balancing his life too. Gilbert, recently a sports broadcaster, carries the sort of charisma and flare that might be seen in the latest romantic comedy film. In their early meetings, Gilbert told Agassi perfectionism might end his career and that perfectionism doesn't exist. Gilbert shared that, with his talent, Agassi didn't need to be perfect to win. A few years later, in contrast, Gilbert told Agassi that because of the shape he was in, he was not giving himself the best chance to win. Gilbert seemed to be good at helping Agassi find his "just right."

Steffi Graf was someone that Agassi admired for years before they became partners and then got married. Graf is considered one of the best female tennis players of all time. When she came into his life, it could be said that it was his phase transition. Like water turning to ice. Physiologic and emotional phase transitions can take weeks or months. Some seem to happen instantaneously. When my daughter brought home her third baby, the older siblings seemed to mature overnight. Agassi gained a stability and alignment toward a purpose that maybe already existed. Graf understood the game, she loved him, and she helped him understand his relationship with the game. After a difficult match, Agassi said, "I hate this game." Graf then replied, "Everyone does." Game, set, match, Mr. Agassi.

Agassi's memoir, *Open*, is a favorite that I have used for years in our resiliency coaching program. It teaches persistence, endurance, perspective, and how love is always in there. His story suggests that with subtle changes in perspective, experiences or moments that seem horrible or undesirable can become the best part of our life. How we each change our perspective is likely to be different from Agassi or our client with leg pain. Knowing that we can change our perspective is the biggest step. The first step usually has to do with others: doing for them, thinking about them, and aligning your purpose to them. Loving them.

POISE(D)

Georges St-Pierre was a renowned mixed martial arts champion, known for having one of the most powerful kicks in the profession. His kicks were often delivered to an opponent's head. Therefore, when performing one of these kicks, St-Pierre not only had to be standing on one leg but also pivoting and raising his kicking leg up very high. My colleague and friend Professor Stuart McGill measured St-Pierre's kicks and studied what was involved in his elite level of performance. Stu is a rare academic who has studied the spine and the clinician. With five books and over 240 scientific publications, I am grateful for what he has discovered and how he has helped fill the gap between what back pain patients experience and what they deserve. His work flows forward into the clinician's hands and, more importantly, the clinician's mind.

Professor McGill placed electrodes on St-Pierre's leg and trunk muscles, and then had him perform his kicks. One of the more intriguing findings was how relaxed St-Pierre's muscles were right before he delivered a kick, and that the same distinct relaxation happened right after the kick. McGill demonstrated that St-Pierre's dramatic transition from relaxation to contraction and back to relaxation was part of the reason that his kicks were so explosive. And why he could deliver the kicks again and again with equal power.

McGill did comparable experiments with one of the best golfers in the world and found a similar sequence of relaxation and contraction. Leading right up to contact with the ball, there was extreme relaxation. Then right before contact with the ball, there would be a blast of contraction, followed by near total relaxation again.

If you ask most athletes, they will tell you the same. When they hold a bat, racquet, or club, it is relaxed just before impact. To be completely relaxed ahead of an explosive effort or event requires preparation, practice, and, yes, poise. Poise is defined as graceful and elegant bearing in a person, having a composed and self-assured manner. Poised is to be balanced.

Former professional tennis player Ashley Barty from Australia exemplifies this concept of poise. As she begins her service motion, her hand is so relaxed on the racquet that several fingers are not even wrapped around the grip. Her other hand has just tossed the ball in the air, and her body posture is perfectly balanced and relaxed as she reaches to make contact with the ball. She could be finishing a dance step or trying to see something up in a closet. All this poise and relaxation just before striking the tennis ball for a serve at 120 miles per hour.

Barty creates such force during the serve that her entire body is off the ground. Yet immediately following the explosive event, her hand on the racquet has loosened again. Her body is relaxed and floating in air as if in a ballet or playing on the beach.

Barty did this often and effectively. She won the French Open, Wimbledon, and the Australian Open and became the number-one ranked tennis player in the world. And then she performed one of the most impressive representations of peak contraction to relaxation. In the moment when she was the best in the world and only twenty-five years old, she retired from tennis. Relax, contract, relax.

To execute dynamic activity with precision requires poise before, within, and after the moment. It could be said that life is full of activities and events that require the same. Poise before, within, and after big and not-so-big moments. If we are to have extraordinary strength and power, accuracy and precision, and peace and joy, and be able to do it again and again, we will likely need to really attend to those things that help us stay poised.

TO RELAX

My daughter, one of the wisest people I know and one of my favorite people, said, "I love that! Very cool insight on how relaxation brings power." *How relaxation brings power.* Wow! Her interpretation was spot-on and surfaces relevant clarity. It's all in the relaxation before and after you hit a ball, take a shot, or throw a kick. In fact, relaxing after you contract ensures you will be relaxed before the next effort and contraction. Harnessing relaxation, therefore, is power. McGill, another wise person, has shown this definitively in his research.

There seem to be two constructs related to the poise(d) principle as it relates to movement and/or performance. First would be to relax, then contract (perform the kick or shot), and then relax, *knowingly*. The other would be to relax, contract, relax, *unknowingly*. To perform this continuum, *knowingly* would include most of the events previously discussed: preparing to hit a tennis serve, executing a kick to the head, or shooting a basketball. Non-sport examples could be performing an incision as a surgeon, executing a brush stroke as a painter, or caressing your child as a parent. *Knowingly* implies that you know you are going to be performing a task.

The unknowing movements or performances would be those where you did not know the contraction, reaction, or response was going to be needed. For example, if you were the one receiving the kick to the head, or a tennis shot went the opposite way than you expected, or someone unexpectedly maneuvered to block your basketball shot. Non-sport events might include you unexpectedly having a knife fall off the counter, heading straight toward your bare foot, and you move just in time; a car pulling out in front of you, and you stop just short of collision; or your child starts falling from the chair at the table, and you grab just enough of them to avoid a fall.

Relaxation brings power and it also brings responsiveness. When you are beginning or idling in a state of relaxation, your responsiveness will be faster, sharper, more precise. When you are beginning or idling in a state that is tense or already contracted, your responsiveness will be slower, less coordinated, and often miss the mark. We have all experienced times when we are in sync and when we are not. When we catch things that fall from the table, and when we are bumping into tables and walls. When the game seems to come to us, and when the game seems foreign. The principle of poise(d) is that you can influence your poised times.

Poise is at the crossroads of prowess and childlike mindset. And the more time you spend knowingly poised, the greater your ability to be poised unknowingly. How are you influencing or practicing your prowess? When are you adding childlike activities?

At a very young age and through a relatively short career, Barty got this.

She played soccer and cricket games with her training team right before her tennis matches. Following a deliberate practice model, she held a very tight circle of experts who helped assess and train her physical, mental, and emotional weaknesses. They worked on her weaknesses in a specific way to identify if they were improving. Practice was focused and intense, not too long, and not always fun. They played games within the game of professional sports to keep things in perspective. Prowess development mixed with childlike experiences. No wonder she ended so poised.

Barty seemed to understand that to be poised for the next performance in her life, something she knowingly valued, she needed to relax, knowingly.

TO RECOVER

In the 2021 French Open, Barty injured her groin, making her unable to complete the tournament. But the bigger concern was that it was twenty-one days before Wimbledon: one of the most prestigious and important tournaments of the year and of any tennis player's career. An MRI confirmed that there was a ten-centimeter tear in her adductor muscle, which is one of the upper muscles of the hamstring, often called the groin. Barty, her team, physical trainer, and physical therapist decided they were going to give it a shot to be able to play Wimbledon.

They rented a house in London and spent the next few days doing treatment and exercise and, most importantly, having fun. They had cooking competitions, relaxed with games, and at one point, Barty used a scooter inside the house, gradually putting weight on her leg. Childlike and fun. As Barty made progress, her trainers and therapists continued to be concerned. She was still having trouble bearing weight on the leg and continued to have considerable pain. Her team did not think she would be able to play.

Approximately ten days before the tournament, they got a new MRI. Barty told her team she didn't want to know the details of the scan. Her team told her it had improved and, therefore, they decided to press on. Over the next week Barty's progress was slow. She was playing and practicing at 50 to 75 percent.

During the first match at Wimbledon, she was not at 100 percent and was guarded, but, through grit and cunning, she won the match. The second match was a similar effort where she graded her stress on her body and her injury at about 90 percent of her potential. Again, it was enough to win.

By the third match, she felt as though she wasn't even thinking about the injury anymore and could play freely and at her normal intensity. She would go on to win Wimbledon and start her ascension to number one in the world. Importantly, Barty and her team continued the same relaxed and childlike activities throughout the tournament. She also read spy-thriller novels—seven books in two weeks!

Many wonderful and fascinating elements of Barty's journey are described in her memoir, *My Dream Time*. One of the more relevant lessons for resiliency is what her team told her after the tournament: the second MRI showed only minimal changes to the injury. She still had a ten-centimeter tear in her groin.

There are numerous pain and injury observations within this story. It is likely that Barty's poise before, during, and after her injury is what made the difference, at every stage: before the injury, during the rehab, and returning to performance. Relax. Contract. Relax.

Recent publications suggest 50%–85% of all medical intervention successes are placebo influenced. This does not mean that physical therapy, medications, or surgery are not useful and beneficial. It simply suggests that you, the patient, the individual, play a big role. And, in concert with this story, it's in your best interest to learn what it takes and what you need to do to attain and sustain that poise.

TO WIN

Imagine you are twenty-five years old and you have recently been named the best in the world in your sport. In the last year you have won Wimbledon, the Australian Open, and several other world-class tournaments. You are doing things that few women in the history of tennis have done. At this young age you will be able to make more money and achieve more fame and recognition for many years to come. In today's world of technology, your potential to wield influence and power will be immense. Again, you are number one in the world, and billions of people know you by name. This was the scenario for Barty. And this was the moment that she made the decision to retire from tennis. She wasn't injured or having mental problems. She did it smiling. She knowingly relaxed. Of all her extraordinary performances, in my opinion, this was her most impressive move.

Following our poise(d) principle, to be relaxed or poised ahead of a stressful event will give you the best chance of having a poised and good response, and the best chance for a good outcome. And, the more poised your response, the more likely you are to have immediate relaxation and poise following the stressful event. Barty seemed to want to be poised for the rest of life more than she wanted anything else.

A CIHP client recently exhibited an example of this phenomenon on a smaller scale. Bill was seventy-seven years old and had had some back-related problems for many years. Anytime he did something out of the ordinary, he might be stiff, suffer pain, and be standing crooked for days to weeks. He had been a client for approximately six months and had been very diligent with his breathing, behavior, and awareness exercises. At a family outing, he was barbecuing using a Weber grill. The Weber grill has a unique hook on the top of the lid to allow you to hang the lid on the grill while turning the meats. It is a valuable design for giving you somewhere to put the lid while you tend to the grilling. If you have used this type of grill, you know it is easy to miss hooking the lid onto the grill. When you miss, it's like expecting to have one more step on a staircase but there isn't one. On this occasion, when Bill went to hook the lid on the grill, he missed hooking the lid and went tumbling to the ground and hit a nearby wheelbarrow. Family members rushed to his aid and to gather the meat that scattered from the grill. The meat was spared, and Bill seemed to have only some mild abrasions. Importantly, after such an abrupt fall directly on his back and hip, Bill had no pain or stiffness that night or for the days following. It is most likely that Bill's resiliency was in part due to his built-up stability and relaxation before the fall. He had trained his relaxation, his poise, for the stressful event.

Bill's decision to take the time and effort to do his exercises every day seemed to have paid off. His poise and prowess really showed through. Imagine if he continues to develop this!

Over the years of working with and being around professional and elite athletes, I was often curious why and how certain athletes seem to handle stressful situations better than others. Whether it was healing from an injury or making a game-winning play. My observation was that these individuals, conscious of it or not, deliberately relaxed. They maybe didn't eat the best or do their exercises as prescribed, but they knew how to be at peace. You might call them "no hurry, no worry" kinds of people. If my observations are correct, and if we utilize the framework of the poise(d) principle, they healed from injuries faster and rarely got nervous in big moments because their reservoir for being relaxed was vast. Therefore, when they were called on to contract or respond, it was powerful and potent. And, importantly, they would settle back to relaxing quickly and fully.

It seems that what almost everyone else would have perceived as more was not Barty's desire. To know that is exceptional. To act on it so decisively, to completely relax, is extraordinary.

It is hard to put Barty's decision and response into perspective. She could have had years of fame and fortune and instead she chose "no hurry, no worry." She chose to be poise(d). She chose not to squeeze the glass. I think it will pay off.

IT'S THE HARD THAT MAKES IT GREAT

In his book *David and Goliath*, Malcolm Gladwell classically illustrates the power of learning out of necessity versus learning that comes easy.

He highlights those who are born with a physical or mental compromise, such as a heart condition or dyslexia, going on to do amazing feats—significantly *due to* their disabilities.

Most of us can relate to some time or event that was similar. We pushed through a stressful or tough test or time and were better for it.

Knowing this, it is fascinating that we are often challenged or sad because of our troubles or burdens despite growing evidence that these are likely our *best* times.

How can we keep our attention on the possible benefits of challenging times? How can we be excited when things are going undesirably?

At the institute we employ a practice called the 6 Ps. While there are sometimes more than six, the primary ones are Perception, Pause, Patience, Perspective, Poise, and Persistence. Just recalling these words and their meaning helps us to restart and reframe difficult situations and/or times.

Like learning to ride a bike, if we Pause, even briefly, and gather our senses of what is happening (Perception), apply some measured focus and control (Poise), and stick to it (Persistence) for a period of time (Patience), we will soon be cruising down the path and riding around the bend. Pause is often the hardest to remember and do. And it's apparent that all are often necessary to sustain a good result. For example, if you leave out your Perception of what is happening, you may grind through and figure out how to ride the bike, but you will not likely have a good sense of what to do when you hit a bump.

The application of this practice is helpful for challenges that are common problems: injury, pain, and disease. The practice of 6 Ps may be even more valuable for those challenges of execution and discipline that happen in front of problems: eating vegetables, exercising for vitality, reading, relaxing, learning, and enduring the stress of achievement. Those important things that most of us recognize as hard.

In the classic movie *A League of Their Own*, Jimmy Dugan (Tom Hanks) and Dottie Hinson (Geena Davis) have an encounter at the end of the movie when Hinson is leaving to go be with her husband and she expresses that she just can't play baseball and be a wife too: "It's just too hard!"

Dugan replies, "It's supposed to be hard. It's the hard that makes it great."

COMMITMENT

Digital Minimalism: a philosophy of technology use in which you focus your online time on a small number of carefully selected and optimized activities that strongly support things you value, and then happily miss out on everything else.

This definition is from the book of the same title by Cal Newport. And while there is enough content in this definition to, say, fill a book, I want to focus on the last line.

To "happily miss out" does not mean that everything will be pleasant, ideal, or happy.

Scientifically, it is strongly suggested that meaningless online activity (clicking, texting, interacting with a device) inhibits important processing centers in our brain. That's right, it makes our thinking weak. Also, these habits have been linked to depression, anxiety, and chronic diseases of the brain.

Reducing or removing online activity may mean short-term inconveniences or new experiences like boredom or solitude. It is also likely to increase human conversation and human interaction.

All of these activities—boredom, solitude, and increased conversation and interaction—are linked to processes in the brain that improve cognition, focus, and happiness. Oh, and genius.

Importantly, our current understanding suggests that we not only have to remove ourselves from undesirable technology time, we have to be OK with it.

Until we commit to "happily missing out," we will not likely experience the change we desire. In fact, emotion has the greater impact. If you set your phone down but fret about missing a text or being left out of the group, you will most likely lose both the battle and the war.

There is good reason to believe this underpins most things. From a golf shot to throwing a baseball to our relationships and/or our faith. Superficial, inauthentic commitment to building, planning, and/or practicing your craft, game, and/or life will eventually, if not quickly, end poorly.

To recap: meaningless online activity leads to depression, anxiety, and chronic brain disease. Boredom, solitude, and human interaction leads to focus, happiness, and . . . genius. Pursue meaningful activity and experience. Is your day positioned for and abundant with people and things that are shining? People and things that are authentic, true, and aligned with good things?

This is what I'm committed to, and I will happily miss out on the rest. Wholly. Congruently.

Simple. Hard. Worthy.

Doing what matters will help you get committed.

TRAINING

FLEXIBILITY AND STABILITY OF FOCUS

"If we do nothing to change our emotional pattern of behavior, tomorrow will resemble yesterday in most details except the date."

Moshe Feldenkrais

TWO LISTS

1. On a piece of paper, make two columns and title one column "Important" and the other "Control."
2. List four to five words or very short phrases under each column. Shorter phrases are better. One word is best.

   - "Important" words should reflect what is important to you. For example, family, friends, faith.
   - "Control" words should reflect what is under your control. For example, your response, your attention, your attitude.

Refer to these lists when questions or situations arise, to help with decisions, choices, and what is worth your attention or stress. With use it will become reflexive.

FOR WORDS

Choose good words. Change your life. Good words are those that move you forward and prompt the mind to look for solutions or choices. For example, when you say "I had a bad day," your mind goes to those images and experiences that are representative of bad and ends there. Your mind will not look for answers. It will not move forward. Versus if you say "I had a challenging day," your mind is prompted toward images and words representing how you could solve this challenge or make it less challenging. Fill your vocabulary with enthusiastic and resourcefulness-building words such as "fascinating," "brilliant," "curious," "undesirable," "not ideal," "lovely." Like many of our recommended trainings, this must be diligently and consistently applied. Commit to having no unhealthy or negative words come out of your mouth. Then, before you know it, it is just how you operate. When you do use an undesirable word, it's only in a situation that warrants it. Otherwise, why give them any attention?!

You are swimming against the current as there are two to three times the negative or undesirable words to positive ones. You will know you are making progress with your vocabulary transformation when your family and/or colleagues start noticing your consistency and positive nature. It's exciting when, often unknowingly, they start doing *the same.*

READING

Reading's value is well recognized and, as many of these evident truths are, underutilized and not often practiced. And like words, what you read can make a difference. Choose your reading material based on your current purpose target and alignment. Choose constructive reading. This does not necessarily mean what is popular or trending. There is high competition for your reading choice: approximately eight hundred books published per day!

Perhaps create a reading club of like-minded individuals. Or identify a circle of advisors to help you select your reading. The Goldilocks principle applies to reading too. Reading works best if it is hitting the "just right" target.

I recommend that you read for an allotted time each day. It can be ten minutes or thirty minutes or more. Make the commitment target feasible in the beginning. As you stick to it, you will likely want to read more. The more you know, the more you want to know. You will notice that your vocabulary increases the more you read. You will communicate better when you read. You will be more present during the day.

Use real books. Read aloud sometimes.

Audio books and Kindle are OK. Some reading is better than none.

If you use technology, mix the real thing in intermittently.

A favorite author and thinker, Professor James Schall, wrote, "To be in a room of 100 books that you have read is an extraordinary thing."

Go for the extraordinary.

ORDERED MORNINGS

Much has been said about instilling order in our lives. We crave it, love it, and, somehow, we often forget to put it on our "important" and "control" lists.

The start of your day is one of the best times to control your order of doing what matters.

Commit to three, five, or sixty minutes that will become your ritual.

I get up at 5:30 a.m., feed our dogs, make my espresso, go to my red chair, pray, read daily spiritual reading, read from a current book, and complete my neuromusculoskeletal (NMS) hygiene.

Saint Augustine of Hippo said, "The definition of peace is the tranquility of order." Peace and its tranquility of order are at the intersection of the 6 Ps.

It is suggested that a ritual is worthy if it is meaningful.

Commit to your ritual.

"This is what I do."

PAUSE TRAINING

One of the most important Ps in our behavior targets has to be "Pause."

If we pause before saying, doing, or even thinking undesirable things, we will often do something better and desirable. Doing something desirable clearly leads to better responses and outcomes.

Practicing pauses is very achievable and, like most things, will lead to a habit forming that carries over to your life events, often without you realizing.

Many deliberate pauses can and often have a secondary benefit. One example of a pause you can take is coloring. Taking three to five minutes to do some coloring creates a pause in your usual activities and has relaxation benefits too. Coloring can produce what is recognized as diffuse brain activity, comparable to daydreaming. It is the "don't try so hard" for the brain. Yes, don't squeeze the glass.

This type of diffuse brain activity occurs when you take a shower. So many great ideas and solutions come forward in the shower because we enter diffuse-thinking mode and are not squeezing the glass so hard.

It is important to randomly mix these intervals of pause in during the day or night. Or at least do them within different activities or events.

Of course, juggling can serve as a deliberate pause and has significant secondary benefits. See Training in part II.

I am sure some of you are already thinking how sensory awareness explorations can be mixed into pause practice. During a social event or lecture, or while doing your homework or preparing for or during serious conversation, deliberate pauses can be implemented. As with all of your tools, the more you practice, the easier it is to sprinkle them into many aspects of your life.

There are likely few things better to help you gain prowess than to do more pausing.

One more thing: when you deliberately practice and execute pausing, a common side effect is listening. Another valued behavior linked to success, happiness, and elite performers.

PART IV

LETTING GO – PHYSICAL AND MENTAL

"A boat is a sensitive thing . . . if it isn't let go free, it doesn't work for you."

George Pocock

KNOW PAIN. KNOW GAIN.

"This week has been a game changer! I have been able to learn more about why I have pain, and now I know I can control my pain and can recover." This was said by a forty-one-year-old mother of three from Ohio. She had suffered sciatica for over two years and had been told her only way to recover was to have surgery. During her visit with us, she learned through movement and education that she could decrease and affect her pain. We see this more and more with our clients who have been suffering: the more they learn about pain, the less pain they have.

Let's repeat that: the more knowledge you have about pain, the less pain you will have. Our clinical work supports this, and so does the current science. A recent study on three hundred patients who had recovered or improved significantly from persistent pain showed that 100% of those consumers felt that knowledge about pain was the most important reason for their recovery. These individuals had suffered with pain for at least five years. Like our client from Ohio, learning why they had pain and that they could control it was a "game changer."

Pain is protective. Pain is directly related to healing. When you touch a hot stove, strain your back, strain your knee, or develop appendicitis, the pain that is produced is designed to protect you so that healing can occur. The pain will persist if you keep touching the stove, continue stressing your back or knee, or don't resolve the inflammation in your appendix. However, once healing has occurred, the pain should subside. Its purpose is complete. That is why it is essential to have practitioners who have knowledge about pain and who can help you identify when healing has occurred. When healing has occurred and you are safe to move, it is usually more dangerous to *not* move than to move. Having practitioners who have knowledge about pain and understand how to help individuals get back to moving and living for their purpose is priceless.

Pain is complicated. Professor Mark Hutchinson, a renowned pain and molecular scientist from Australia, states, "There are more cellular interactions in one pain event than . . . stars in the universe." Pinch your arm enough to produce some mild pain. The signal from your arm to your spinal cord involves the billions of cellular interactions Hutchinson is talking about. Importantly, these interactions—communications from one cell to another—involve cells of the nervous system as well as the immune system. This means that most pain involves our immune system, and our immune system is involved in most of our pain. This strongly connects pain to health and health to pain.

We have a lot to gain by knowing more about pain. With neurons and immune cells being intimately linked, improving pain occurrence impacts overall health. Concurrently, approximately 75% of all days of disability in the world are attributed to pain. Therefore, if we as a society become more knowledgeable about pain, and reduce our occurrence and improve recovery of pain, we will be more productive and save our communities billions of dollars.

It seems intuitive to have "no" pain. The reality is that relentlessly pursuing absolutely no pain is one of the most likely ways to have more pain. And in this way, "no pain equals no gain."

In *Shadowlands*, a movie about C. S. Lewis's relationship with an American writer who would eventually become his wife, there is a poignant message on pain. Joy, C. S. Lewis's wife, played by Debra Winger, reflects the direct connection of the physical and emotional aspects of pain. In the story, she has bone cancer, and after some improvement with treatment, it relapses with a likely fatal outcome. Lewis, played by Anthony Hopkins, displays anger and frustration with the amount of pain she experiences and the pain of losing her. Winger attempts to assure him by relating that suffering is part of the deal and suffering is part of the happiness now.

Winger's message in the movie is based on a quote from the book that C. S. Lewis wrote after Joy's death: "The pain I feel now is the happiness I had before. That's the deal."

Pain is part of the deal. In fact, it is an amazing asset. There is a resiliency transformation that occurs when an individual endures and learns from suffering and pain. From my experience in dealing with elite athletes and complicated pain conditions for over twenty years, it can be one of the best things that can happen to you. The earlier in your life you can learn about pain and suffering, the better you will be. Look at high achievers, survivors, and leaders—most have endured hardship in their life. Often, at a young age.

In *The Book of Charlie*, David Von Drehle artfully recaps the life of Charlie White, who lived 109 years. He chose White because of the way White lived those 109 years. Drehle saw remarkable resilience in White and his nearly being a supercentenarian. In his history, like so many others like him who do extraordinary things, White had a personal tragedy at a young age where he had to rise up. He led a wonderful and long life, and pain was part of the deal. Increasing your knowledge about pain and learning during experiences with pain will help you believe in your capacity to control your pain, resiliency, and health. Yes, it's an important training ground for self-efficacy. Knowledge and understanding of pain will help you see, feel, and appreciate your happiness now.

GO THE DISTANCE

The following stories on competitive runners are intended to surface the knowledge for life that can be discovered through their experiences. You may be curious how distance running is related to you or resilience. Make no mistake, these stories are about you and me and the teams around us. Big and small teams that assist us with the races of our lives. Distance running requires commitment, endurance, and stamina. It calls on responsiveness, grit, and other character traits we have previously discussed: Perception, Pause, Patience, Perspective, Poise, and Persistence. To be a world-class runner you need physical ability, mental tenacity, and hard work. To have world-class resiliency you need the same. It is often said, "Life is a marathon, not a sprint." The more appropriate quote might be "Life is a marathon and sometimes a sprint."

PART IV: LETTING GO

BREAKING YOU

Are you finding it difficult to lose weight? Are you finding it's taking longer to accomplish your fitness goals than you expected? Are you thinking your pain should be gone by now?

Back in 2015, Nike decided to sponsor an attempt to beat the two-hour record for the marathon. Nike selected three elite marathon runners and surrounded them with a twenty-person team of designers, engineers, coaches, and physiologists. Millions of dollars later, the attempt took place in Monza, Italy, selected for being the perfect altitude and temperature, on May 6, 2017. The documentary by *National Geographic* is available on Amazon Prime Video and numerous streaming channels. It is worth the fifty-five minutes to get the full appreciation of everything that went into this project and to experience Eliud Kipchoge. Kipchoge is one of the elite runners and is an important part of this story. He was the fastest of the three in the race; however, he went twenty-five seconds past the two-hour mark. Kipchoge said after the race, "Now the next 26 seconds will be easier."

And in fact, two years later, with another team of designers, engineers, coaches, and physiologists, hundreds of supportive staff, and millions of dollars, Kipchoge did break the two-hour barrier, and ran the marathon in 1 hour 59 minutes and 40 seconds.

In the *Breaking2* documentary, Kipchoge references how the race is won with the heart and the mind and not the legs. An extraordinary perspective from a marathon runner! Kipchoge's humility and poise are admirable. His appreciation of the value of his team is brilliant and refreshing.

For an elite athlete to perform a feat that he had never done before, it required a twenty-person team, unlimited resources, and time. Four years! And he did everything to the letter. This sounds like *doing what matters*!

When we are trying to make physiologic changes—lose weight, improve strength, change pain—it usually requires a similar equation: resources, a team, and time.

You have come this far in your race; the next twenty-six seconds will be easier.

RACE OF A LIFETIME

By 1885, the fastest human mile recorded was four minutes and twenty seconds. By 1940, that had been eclipsed at four minutes and two seconds. And then, though many tried, that did not change for over ten years. Individuals ran the mile in four minutes and seven seconds, four minutes and six seconds, four minutes and nine seconds, and many other combinations. Four minutes seemed to be a natural limit. Like water freezing at 32°F.

It was thought that running a mile in under four minutes was impossible. Medical and performance studies supported the biological conclusion that this was outside the physiologic capabilities of man.

In 1952, Roger Bannister was an Olympic gold medal favorite for the fifteen-hundred-meter race in Helsinki, Finland. Like most Olympic athletes, he had trained for three years for this event. Unlike most, he had trained using his own unique methods and without a coach. There was criticism of his approach. Yet, due to his previous success, he was still the projected favorite to win. He came in fourth. By all accounts, he failed.

At this time, Bannister was in the middle of his medical school training and considered shelving his running and athletic career. Instead, in less than a month's time, he decided to continue running and competing. On May 6, 1954, he ran the mile in three minutes and fifty-nine seconds. He became one of the most heralded runners and athletes of all time.

An underrecognized aspect of Bannister's feat of running a mile under four minutes is that he overcame this seemingly impossible barrier while he was in fact studying biology to become a doctor of neurology. To help put this into perspective, during this time period, women giving birth were hospitalized and isolated from their babies and families for usually at least ten days, there was no surgery for repairing the heart, and it was well established that the mind and body were separate and distinct. Bannister was swimming against the social and science culture that had pronounced running a sub-four-minute mile unattainable. And, it is likely that this was why and how he did it.

Is there anything you think is impossible? Have you and others been attempting these feats for a long time, perhaps years, without success? Is it culturally accepted that these barriers are normal and not reachable?

JOY

Four minutes. The time it takes to get a cup of coffee at Starbucks. The equivalent to sitting through a long stoplight. The time it takes to toast a piece of bread or to complete two sets of incline presses with a sixty-second rest. The amount of time to read a blog.

Imagine running a mile in this amount of time.

To accomplish this feat requires extraordinary performance. Almost twice as many individuals have climbed to the top of Mount Everest than have run a mile in under four minutes.

Bannister's approach to training was his own. He remembered the specific moment of exhilaration and freedom he felt as a youth when running on the beach. His confidence in it was reinforced by Gunder Hägg's training diary on the fartlek (speed play) method. Hägg had been a world record holder for the mile. His training alternated gentle running with fast running over distances from one hundred yards to a mile. The aim was to give speed and stamina to the athlete, imitating the games children play on the playground involving short bursts of running breathless, followed by a pause for recovery. Many of Bannister's competitors attempting to break the four-minute mile were using complex systems of training. Bannister chose simplicity versus complexity. Bannister's approach was clearly aligned with the joy and sensation of running above most anything else.

Bannister later related that attempts to analyze running always fell short. He said they were "like the description of a rose to someone who has never seen one." I love this perspective, and while Bannister relates it to running, it likely relates to many aspects of sport, training, and life.

After his loss at the Helsinki Olympics, Bannister had several running colleagues and a new coach who helped in his pursuit of the four-minute mile. The coach did not dictate his approach but supported it. In this way, Bannister followed a deliberate practice platform: identify specific areas of weakness (aided by experts in the field), practice those areas intently and intensely, reassess progress with experts in the field, and repeat, deliberately practicing more.

Bannister and his teammates trained for two years. He and some friends decided to take a break due to stagnation in their performance times just three weeks out from the race where Bannister set the world mark. They went climbing in Scotland. After a ten-hour cramped car ride, they climbed hard elevations for three days. "Using all the wrong muscles all the wrong ways," Bannister would later say. After returning from their climbing, Bannister's running times reached the levels needed to break the record. Maybe it was the physiologic change in training, or maybe it was the emotion and environment in the mountains. Or was it the rekindling of the joy he experienced as a child? Or perhaps both?

What could be your *four minutes*?

MEANING

Josef Pieper, a twentieth-century philosopher, wrote, "Words convey reality."

Bannister was consistent with his own words and strategy. He often referred to joy, courage, and meaningful experiences in his descriptions of how and why he ran.

Bannister exhibited resiliency and self-efficacy at many points during his racing career. As a youth, he was small and sometimes would get bullied. At age eleven, although smaller than most of his competitors, he won a two-mile cross-country race. In several autobiographies, Bannister remembered how he could run to exhaustion and push himself more than others. His schoolyard problems halted due to his success in running. Bannister saw this as a gift to him, he said, "As if by magic."

A client once said to me, "This Bannister guy doesn't look like he lifted weights." I replied, "Probably not. Training, culture, and the environment were a little different then." During the majority of Bannister's running career, over ten years, his country was either in the middle of a world war or recovering from it. He trained and competed in a country that was rationing its food. Britain ended its rationing program in 1954, the year he performed the sub-four-minute mile.

Bannister chose to compete for the record on a day when the weather was at its worst. On the train ride up to Oxford for the race where he would break the record, he happened to be sitting by Franz Stampfl, the coach who had worked with him over the past year. As Bannister boarded the train, he was undecided as to whether he would run for the record. Windy and rainy in the 1950s meant that the cinder-and-dirt track would be very different and difficult compared to today's synthetic track. There were no covered stadiums. Undesirable weather created real change and obstacles. Stampfl said he thought

Bannister could break four minutes in good and bad weather. Bannister seemed to use this moment and these words as permission to *believe* that he could succeed. And he did. Perhaps a moment of self-efficacy.

Bannister overcame many obstacles: physical, emotional, environmental, and cultural. He believed in his joy of running and persisted, at least partly, to reward those who had been loyal and supported him along the way. In many instances Bannister's explorations and discoveries appeared not to be a *result* of his running, but the very *purpose* of his running.

Steve Prefontaine, the next runner's story, thought by many to be one of the greatest distance runners of all time, said, "To give anything less than your best is to sacrifice the gift."

Bannister's development and use of his gift was extraordinary, and he seemed to be sincerely grateful. Woven throughout his success formula were meaningful pursuits that supported the strategy of being aligned with purpose and belief. The story is our gift. What will you do with it?

PRE-WILL

Steve Prefontaine has been referred to as America's greatest running legend. What he achieved in a relatively short career is impressive. *How* he achieved it is *why* it was and remains extraordinary.

For five years, no American runner could beat Steve Prefontaine at any distance over a mile. He owned every American record (eight) between two thousand and ten thousand meters and between two miles and six miles. He also held eight collegiate records while at the University of Oregon, with his three-mile (12:53.4) and six-mile (27:09.4) standing for over twenty years.

He held more American records than any other male track athlete in history.

Known by his fans as "Pre," Steve Prefontaine was the first athlete to be paid by Nike to wear their shoes and is the only athlete to have a statue on the campus in Oregon. While there are no statistics on this occurrence, it is said that the sun often broke through the clouds when Pre came onto the track.

Pre often took the lead in his races. He sometimes led through the whole race and frequently won the race by a lot. This is commonly called a front-runner. Tactically, this is a disadvantage. The runner in front breaks the wind for the runners behind them. Many distance runners plan their bursts of sprinting and only move to the front at specific times. Most distance runners draft or let others break the wind until the end of the race and then sprint to the finish. Pre's intent was to give his all the whole race. Fans loved it. His coaches did not.

Bill Bowerman, Pre's first coach at the University of Oregon, tried to get Pre to change his strategy of running in the front. Bowerman rarely had success in changing Pre's approach. Later Bowerman would say, "That man was made to run away with things." Walt McClure, Pre's high school coach, described Pre as someone who could control his fatigue and pain. McClure said, "His threshold is different than most of us." McClure wasn't sure if this was inborn or if Pre developed it himself.

Pre was known to train as intensely as he raced. Few could keep up with his training routines, and if they did, he would make sure they could not for long. In four years at the university, he never missed a workout or track meet due to illness or injury. At the 1970 NCAA championships, Pre got a gash on his right foot requiring twelve stitches. Three days later, with a bloody foot, he won the five-thousand-meter, and Oregon won the championship.

At the midpoint of his running career, Pre and some of the best runners in America were assessed for their physiologic capacities. At the time, this testing facility had tested some of the top athletes in the world. Pre knew this and therefore made the decision to have the best score on the test. His VO2 max—the maximum amount of oxygen an individual can use during intense or maximal exercise—was the top of his group, and only a few athletes in the world at that time had ever tested higher. During the psychological part of the test, Pre revealed his philosophy about racing. He qualified that it was not just about winning but about seeing who had the most guts. This opinion of running competition also carried over to how he ran the race. What was reported on several occasions was his comment "To let someone else lead the whole way and then try to steal the race at the end is chickenshit."

C. S. Lewis said, "If you look for truth, you may find comfort in the end; if you look for comfort you will not get either comfort or truth—only soft soap and wishful thinking to begin and, in the end, despair."

It seems Pre looked for truth in how and why he raced and in other aspects of his life that we will cover in the coming segments. And, although sometimes he was viewed to be overconfident and abrasive, his views were transparent and truthful as he saw it. Refreshingly, he certainly never looked for comfort. His authenticity to give his best, to do what he saw as the right way to go about using your gift, was maybe the reason he was so admired back then and today.

In "The Grit," we will look at those times when he did not win.

THE GRIT

A CIHP team leader asked, "Maybe the equation that the Pre story suggests is Gift + Grit = Greatness?" A very clever insight and question.

Prefontaine said, "I do it because I can. I can because I want to. I want to because you said I couldn't."

An individual's resiliency and performance often run parallel paths and are both defined by bell curves where too much or too little can come up short. Applying the Goldilocks principle, similar to early stages of recovery, when you move toward the edges of excellence, the line between success and failure can become very thin. What makes us great can also cause us harm. Ingredients and efforts that have the potential for dramatic and exceptional positive effects can often also have undesirable ones. In areas that are undiscovered—running faster than any other human, healing an incurable disease, or simply identifying good stresses—exploration and discovery are required. This, of course, has risks. It takes courage. You cannot be chickenshit. It sometimes has costs.

By the end of his second year at the University of Oregon, Pre had lost some races. Most of those losses were to Europeans or in races that were shorter distances than his specialties.

What was impressive over his career was that Pre would run races, like the mile, against runners who specialized in the mile. Even though he was not a miler—his specialty was the five-thousand-meter and three-mile—he ran the mile under four minutes in ten different races. It seemed Pre ran these disadvantaged races because they were a challenge, to support a cause, or, most often, for the loyalty that he felt to those fans and people who had supported him over the years.

In the 1972 Olympics, he qualified to compete with a very experienced field of runners in the five-thousand-meter race. There was anticipation, especially in the United States, that Pre could win the race. Pre's televised statement leading up to the race was a classic example of his confidence and style. Pre said, "I hope the race comes down to who has the most guts. If it does, I think I have a pretty good chance."

Pre did not run his usual race. He did not take the lead until the last mile of a three-mile race. It seemed he was trapped inside some of the more experienced runners. In the last lap, the lead changed between Pre and Lasse Virén from Finland several times. During the sprint in the last turn, he was cut off by another runner. Pre could not regain his momentum; the other runners passed him in the last fifty yards. Pre placed fourth. Many of Pre's peers would say that he ran the best race they had ever seen him run up to that point.

This defeat staggered Pre, but only for a moment. When the spring season started only a few months later, he re-started his habit of first-place finishing and record breaking. Bowerman said, "He didn't lose too many, but when he did, he would bounce back." Pre began to modify his approach and to listen to Coach Bowerman and Coach Bill Dellinger. He never fully relinquished his all-out intensity and, most of all, his desire for racing and competing above winning.

Mihaly Csikszentmihalyi was a psychologist well known for his work in the field of human performance. He identified the mental state called "flow," of which he wrote a book by the same title. He defined this state as stretching a person's mind or body to its limit in a voluntary effort to accomplish something difficult or worthwhile.

Pre's ability to stretch his body and mind to the limit is likely what he most cherished about competing and running. Some might say Pre lived in a state of flow. His challenge, and maybe some of ours, was to balance that wonderful feeling and reward of pushing things to the limit with the prowess and capacity to finish the race.

The equation might be Gift + Grit + Guidance = Sustained Greatness.

THE GIFT

Among his many unique philosophies, Pre believed that physical training could solve many of the world's problems. This was part of his mission and work with Nike and youth athletes. An example of this approach was his 6:00 a.m. ten-mile run that he rarely missed. He used it to rejuvenate himself through sheer effort. To resolve fatigue, pain, or the flu.

A CIHP team leader asked, "Could the type and prolonged amount of grit and intensity that Steve Prefontaine maintained lead to future problems or injury?" In other words, when is too much of a good thing too much?

Over the years of working with elite athletes, from professional baseball to ballet to military, the average age they show up at the institute has been twenty-seven years old. They often move through their early years training hard, competing intensely, and with minimal pain or injury. I would commonly hear them say, "I was never injured in high school or college." They seem invincible until they are not.

The resiliency built by Pre is one that should be studied and pursued. His approach consisted of having something he wanted to do, someone to do it for, and a congruent belief he could do it. As simple as this seems, many athletes and nonathletes lack this. Congruency and clarity being the most common missing pieces. It is a formula for succeeding during a career, recovering from injury or disease, or getting on to the next game.

While potent and often essential for shifting health and performance, this unrelenting attention and/or "will" to succeed works best with conscious and consistent restraint. In one of my favorite movies, *Dead Poets Society*, Professor Keating (Robin Williams) tells his students, "Sucking the marrow out of life doesn't mean choking on the bone."

In 1975, at the age of twenty-four, Pre had restored his running to what some say was his highest level. Despite injuries and sciatica, he won all five of the races he ran. With the 1976 Montreal Olympics in his sights, he set a new American record in the two-thousand-meter in his hometown of Coos Bay, Oregon. The evening of the last race of that month, the NCAA preparatory race leading up to Olympic trials, Prefontaine was killed in a car accident.

In a late-night, poorly understood one-car accident, Steve Prefontaine was gone.

He would not get to compete again in the Olympics or any other race.

Kenny Moore, Pre's teammate and coauthor of the movie *Without Limits*, said at Pre's eulogy, "Many of us will say, 'I had no idea how much that man meant to me,' due to not knowing how much we meant to him."

I would wager that if you spend any time with Prefontaine's story, you will absorb Moore's message. You will find yourself standing and cheering like the rest of us.

After tragic and sudden deaths, especially if the individual took up a big space, there is often an attempt to analyze the meaning or message. Could something have been done? Or, what can we learn? The misguided temptation is thinking that he or we deserved more.

Perhaps the days Prefontaine lived were enough. Maybe the lesson is that at the crossroads of competing, living, and courage is a joy that is not always pleasant. Maybe what leaves us curious is the best thing.

THE ART OF INDIFFERENCE

Molly Seidel is not quite a legend like the previous runners, Bannister and Prefontaine, yet she has performed some legendary feats. The first time in her life she ran twenty-six miles, the distance of the marathon, was in the 2020 Olympic trials, when she qualified for the team by coming in second place. In only her third marathon race, she won an Olympic bronze medal. Only three American women have ever medaled in the Olympic marathon, and 2004 was the last time this had happened. In her fifth marathon, she ran the fourth-fastest time ever by a woman in the New York City Marathon and set a new American record for that course.

Seidel caught my attention because of *how* she won the Olympic medal in 2021. My fortune was that I just happened to be tuned in to the finish of the women's marathon. I think there were several things that pulled me in and kept me watching to see what happened. It was clear that the announcers had not planned on Seidel being in third position with the other elite runners. The broadcasters seemed unprepared and were genuinely surprised by what was happening. One of them said, "She is running with experience, quite frankly, that she doesn't have."

She held on and got third, a bronze medal. And then, what reeled me in and prompted my desire to learn more about this story was her comments immediately after the race.

She said, "I am so tired." She praised the talent of the runners she raced with. She expressed gratitude for all of her team and family. "I figured if I just stuck with those really talented runners, stuck my nose where it didn't belong and just kind of was brave, something good might come from it." She did not praise herself. Then with tears in her eyes, she asked her family to drink a beer for her.

Seidel seemed sincere, humble, and unaffected by the extraordinary feat she had performed. As I will cover in the next two parts of this story, Seidel had plenty of emotional and physical challenges to overcome. She had high expectations, an eating disorder, and several serious and chronic injuries. Her journey, like most of ours, was full of ups and downs and, sometimes, despair.

Her perceived indifference during her interview as to what was expected or what she could control might have been the ingredient that helped her overcome previous difficulties related to running and life. And it might have been the ingredient that had her performing with experience that she didn't have.

Hold on for a fun ride with a joyful young woman from Wisconsin who won races and hearts and had some experiences that may help us all be indifferent to those things that are "none of our business."

TO HARDSHIP

This is one of my favorite G. K. Chesterton quotes: "Courage is almost a contradiction in terms . . . A soldier surrounded by enemies, if he is to cut his way out, needs to combine a strong desire for living with a strange carelessness about dying . . . He must seek his life in a spirit of furious indifference to it; he must desire life like water and yet drink death like wine."

Molly Seidel grew up in Wisconsin. She is from the Midwest. Maybe that is why I like her. Maybe that is why most of the world likes her. Three of the principles her mom always told her were don't quit, don't look behind you, and don't cheat. While her marathon success came out of nowhere, her running career did not.

She established her running prowess in grade school. At the first cross-country event she entered, she threw up before the race and did not compete. A few weeks later she entered another race and won. In seventh grade she ran for the Saint Joan of Arc School track team. Of course she did.

Her humble surroundings allowed her to develop her athletic talents without too much attention. Seidel repeated over several recent interviews that she was very grateful for her early environment. Her family, the culture, and early coaches really helped her when things got more difficult and complicated later in her career.

In 2011, her senior year of high school, Seidel was named Gatorade National Female Cross Country Runner of the Year and won the Foot Locker Cross Country Championship. This is a very distinguished US championship where the top forty elite runners from across the United States are invited to compete in a 3.1-mile race. Before Seidel, no US woman who had won the Foot Locker Championship had gone on to win an Olympic medal.

After high school, Seidel made the decision to study and run at the University of Notre Dame. Her first two years there were challenging, and she had little success with her running. She was frequently injured and even came in last in one of her races. Her junior year a new coach arrived, and a new Seidel surfaced. She would go on to win six national championship races in the five-thousand-meter and ten-thousand-meter (3.1 and 6.2 miles).

In 2016, her senior year at Notre Dame, she won four national championship races and was given the Honda Sports Award for top female cross-country runner. She says of that time, "I was maybe the unhappiest I had ever been." Instead of signing a lucrative professional contract, Seidel checked herself in to a rehab center for eating disorders.

At that time, Seidel related that she was very close to

quitting. She shared that her mom said, "I will love you if you never run again. I will love you if you decide to run again."

She decided to run again, she said, because "it's where I fit in." She talked about having OCD and said that when she was out there running and racing, she was actually the most comfortable.

In several interviews, Seidel stated that, while she was in a deep hole with her eating disorder, she found peace by realizing she doesn't have to be perfect. She relayed that she had learned to take running less seriously. In a wonderful final comment, she stated, "It's not rocket science, it's running."

Once Seidel turned pro in 2017, she was still suffering with injuries at the end of her first year. She found out she had an unhealed fracture in her pelvis that she had been running on for about a year. She was told she had to have surgery and that she might not be able to run competitively again. Once more, Seidel's decision to continue running meant a lot of hardship, suffering, and hard work. She said she was close to quitting. She did not.

In 2019, Seidel made a change to work with a new coach and, as part of that decision, to run longer distances. She excelled in that approach and at a rooftop party decided to compete in the trials for the Olympic marathon even though she had never run that distance. Ever.

In a pre–Olympic trials interview, Seidel was asked about the twenty-third mile being the toughest for a marathon race. At that time, she had never been to the twenty-third mile in a race. She said her approach was going to be, simply, to "send it!" Seidel stated she was not much into visualization or planning. She added, "What do they say, if you want to make God laugh, make a plan."

Another pretty good clutch performer, Michael Jordan, once said, "Why would I worry about the shots I haven't taken yet?"

Seidel had never run the marathon distance before competing in the Olympic trials marathon. She got second.

TO SECURE CARELESSNESS

Former Navy SEAL and current congressman Dan Crenshaw said, "In difficulty, in adversity, in *meaningful* suffering—there is transformation." He had personal history to support his beliefs. Crenshaw had one eye blown away and the other severely damaged by an enemy explosive in Afghanistan. After several surgeries and years of recovery, he not only regained his eyesight but rejoined his SEAL unit, went on to get a master's degree, and is now a congressman. He commented that when the doctors said, "It's virtually impossible that you will regain your eyesight," he focused on one word: "virtually." Crenshaw was seemingly indifferent to any possibility that he would never see again.

Comparatively, Seidel had experienced stress fractures to her tibia, fibula, pelvis, sacrum, and ribs. She had suffered depression, anxiety, and mental illness starting at age sixteen.

Does it take a certain amount of suffering to attain the quality of indifference necessary to have extraordinary success? Or is your perspective and alignment of purpose during and after suffering what matters?

The application of indifference is not new. The Stoics practiced it, Special Operations military professionals imbibe it, and many religions have it as their cornerstone. Boiled down, the proposed action is focusing tenaciously on those things you can control and relentlessly avoiding those things you cannot. With practice this leads to responding to moments and events versus reacting. Gaining poise and prowess minimizes vulnerability, fragility, and defeat.

There can be a fine line between indifference as a vice versus a virtue. Individuals with indifference related to meaningful pursuits will often be noticeably authentic, humble, and pleasant. Think James Braddock, Eliud Kipchoge, or your favorite uncle, aunt, or grandparent. Versus those who are indifferent related to nonmeaningful pursuits, things, or titles, who will often exhibit a character that is inauthentic, arrogant, and aloof. Think Gordon Gekko, Mr. Potter, or professional athletes who celebrate and praise themselves during the game.

In one of Seidel's pre–Olympic trials interviews, she seemed very poised and ready to run a race she had never run. At the same time, she was very humble and praised those who were more experienced than her. In this interview, she mentioned her approach of "sending it." She acknowledged that her race might be flawed but that no matter how hard it got, she was going to just send it. More subtly she shared, "Nothing else gets in." Like Bannister and Prefontaine, a "secure carelessness" on the precipice of the impossible.

Notably, the main difference between Seidel's pre–Olympic trials interview in 2020 and her post–Olympic medal interviews in 2021 was an Olympic medal and three marathon races. Her personality, humility, and joy were, remarkably, the same. Kind of neat.

In an interview after the New York City Marathon, her fourth marathon, where she set a new American women's record and after the race identified that she did it with two broken ribs, she summarized how she loved the preparation and nature of the marathon. She recognized how grueling it was and that she might train upward of 130 miles a week! From her language and her expression, it seemed like she had found her race. Again, speaking about the marathon, she said, "It just kind of sets my soul on fire."

Over a significant period of time, through her suffering and a lot of hard work, Seidel surfaced new meaning in and around her running. Through this discovery it seems she was capable of being indifferent in ways that went well beyond her experience. Indifferent to anything not aligned with her currently recognized meaning and/or purpose—what was truly important and in her control.

I am convinced that there is something that can set everyone's soul on fire. For a very, very small percentage it is running or racing in a marathon. The beauty is knowing it exists. There can be multiple things and ways to experience them. Being indifferent to thoughts that finding and/or mastering what sets your soul on fire is easy or expedient can be the art that some are missing. It cannot burn bright all the time. There will be seasons of sunshine, wind, rain, and drought.

Once you find what sets your soul on fire, you can get to work at mastering it for the rest of your life.

HARD AS A CHOICE

The song "Iris" by the Goo Goo Dolls has a lyric about bleeding to know you are alive.

This has always been one of those lyrics that I sing out loud. The rest of the song is very good, but this lyric is what I sing along with loudly anytime I hear the song. Most of us have those. Often in a car alone or even sometimes with a crowd.

This lyric resonates due to the link to resiliency. The intersection of fear and recovery, the crossroads of failure and success. It is at the edge that you find your edge.

Many of the baseball players that I worked with would deliberately work to develop calluses in spring training. The hitters would develop them on their hands for swinging the bat. The pitchers would develop them on their fingers for throwing the ball. Calluses develop when the skin is exposed to repetitive stresses or irritation for a long period of time. While the tissues that make up the callus are dead, the hardened mass is resistant to mechanical or chemical damage. Calluses thus become protective. If the players failed to sufficiently develop the calluses for the season to come, they would be battling blisters and soreness all season. Blisters and soreness would not only be undesirable but would lead to poor performance and possibly problems in the wrist, elbow, and shoulder. Poor performance, for many, was the most dreaded of the possibilities.

The odds of a child who plays Little League baseball to eventually be drafted into the major leagues is approximately 0.0005 percent, or one in two hundred thousand. To play at the major league level, the odds are one in a million. The odds of becoming a Special Forces military professional are approximately 0.0000125 percent, or one in eight million. These types of elite performances, and those even more elite, usually require both physical and mental calluses. In almost every scenario, you will find individuals volunteering again and again to do something difficult, stressful, and unrelenting, like intentionally developing calluses.

This is why doing something hard is essential. Bannister, Prefontaine, and Seidel all used this strategy. Dan Crenshaw—Navy SEAL, war veteran, and congressman—identified that it is best if the hard accomplishment is voluntary. He stated, "Voluntary hardship elicits a different psychological response than involuntary hardship."

There is a neurobehavioral complexity to volunteering to do something hard. The likely result is that the more voluntary hardships you endure, the better you will be prepared for the involuntary ones. And there will be involuntary ones. For most of us, many of them.

How do you develop mental calluses? Enduring difficult moments and experiences is the practice that is required. Including high repetition of stressful events. Volunteering to endure stressful events is hard. If we find ourselves battling the blisters and soreness of events and relationships that are part of playing the game, perhaps we have been avoiding the deliberate practice of doing things that are hard. Maybe we simply have not identified which voluntary hard activity would help us to be stronger. Often aligned with fear, it is natural to resist doing something hard. And, maybe like never before, our culture supports strategies that seem to rebel against and discourage the very thing that would make us stronger—that is, doing something hard.

In life, not developing these calluses could have significant results: poor performance or not being able to play the game, the most undesirable of all. This brings us full circle, back to Eliud Kipchoge, the amazing runner who ran a marathon in under two hours. His quote on his team is worth noting:

"100% of me is nothing compared to 1% of my team." It is likely that our team—family, friends, practitioners, and mentors—is the distinctive difference for those who find courage and its companion, joy. A good team/circle will know the things that are hard, help you to find them, and, with their wisdom and guidance, cheer you through them. Here's to learning how to set your soul on fire.

REST AND CREATING SPACE

Eddie Jaku was a Holocaust and Auschwitz prison camp survivor. He told his story in the wonderful book *The Happiest Man on Earth*. His book was thoughtfully written and certainly goes into the library for resiliency training. There are many valuable lessons from his story.

Jaku was born in Germany and declared that he was German first, German second, and Jewish third. This made the Nazi atrocities that he and his family suffered very disturbing. He could not believe Germans from the country he loved would treat him and his family this way. He was forced to stop going to school at the age of thirteen. His father procured a new identity for him, and he attended a school nine hours from his family under a false identity. At age eighteen, he returned to his German home, and the Nazi police were waiting for him. His faithful dog was killed in front of him, and he was beaten severely and taken to his first prison camp.

After escaping his imprisonment for being Jewish, he was arrested for being German twice and imprisoned by Belgian and French police. Finally, after all of that, he was again imprisoned by the Germans at Auschwitz.

He and his family arrived at Auschwitz together, and his mother and father were killed as soon as they arrived. Jaku was forced to work from 6:00 a.m. to 6:00 p.m. Most days he marched for hours to and from work. In many of his jobs, he wore a sign around his neck that stated if he failed in his task or allowed a machine to stop running, he was to be shot immediately. The people in the camp were treated horrifically, as is well documented. They had poor nutrition, poor housing, and inadequate clothing in frigid temperatures. They were forced to sleep naked in freezing temperatures so that the prisoners would not escape. The beds allowed ten men to a row. It was vital to wake throughout the night to rotate positions because if you were on the outside of the row all night, you would freeze to death. Literally.

After a failed attempt to escape, Jaku needed help getting a bullet out of his leg. He asked a Jewish prisoner he knew was a doctor to help him. The doctor met him privately and removed the bullet from his leg with a butter knife. He then advised Jaku to keep it sanitized with saliva. The leg healed. I told you he was kind of resilient.

Jaku said the doctor gave him advice that saved his life. He told Jaku to rest whenever he could. He told him to lie down. The doctor told Jaku that all the others would be looking for food or clothing or trying to find their family, but he should lie down. He told him that one hour of rest equaled two days of survival.

Jaku escaped from Auschwitz at the end of the war, barely avoiding extermination in the death marches. He was so sick from typhoid and dysentery that the doctors in the hospital gave him a 30 percent chance of surviving. Jaku lived to the age of 101.

Approximately 1.3 million people were sent to Auschwitz. Eighty-five percent of them were murdered at the facility. Many died after escaping, during and after the war.

The doctor's recommendation for Jaku to rest leaps from the story for all of us to hear. Time for recovery is essential. Additionally, it speaks to the idea of providing space for body and mind. Space for good things and thoughts to surface and gain traction.

In his wonderful book, *The Creative Act*, Rick Rubin describes how the best way to hear or see what is hard to define is to not try. He discourages attempts of analysis or prediction. He suggests creating a space that allows it to come in.

Jaku created space by lying down. He did what the doctor recommended and nothing else.

Rubin suggests that the universe is constantly supplying information and ideas and that they will only land with us if we create space. When we free up sufficient space, he says our minds function "as a vacuum."

When you deliberately rest, as Jaku did, you create space for recovery. When you deliberately rest physically and/or mentally, you create a vacuum for good things.

In a TED Talk in 2019, before he passed, Jaku talked about young people today and how they are always commenting on how they are running here and there. Jaku questioned this, saying, "I don't know where they are going!"

At one hundred years of age, Jaku seemed to appreciate the idea of rest and creating space even more. One of my least favorite words, especially around the institute, is "busy." I have for a long time found it undesirable, and, a year ago, I heard a Zen reference for the definition of the word "busy." It stated, "Busy means your heart is full."

This perspective of the word "busy" and others suggests there isn't room for anymore. No room for others or good things. Jaku doesn't know where people are running. Why would you ever want to be busy or say you are busy?

Are you getting enough rest? Sleep is what we first think of when considering rest. And while your sleep is very important, rest achieved in other ways may have as much or more relevance and potency. The rest *between*. The rest between workouts. The rest between sets. The rest between important presentations or projects. The rest between any stressful event and your next step.

What is your survival equation? What is your thriving equation? What does one hour of rest mean for you? What does twenty minutes of reading or three minutes of juggling or coloring equal?

Do you have space in your day? Do you have space in your mind? Do you have space in your heart?

PERFECT FORCE

One of my favorite groups of athletes and people is performing artists. My team and I were blessed to work with some of the world's most talented and recognized performing artists, from the New York City Ballet to Les Grands Ballets Canadiens de Montréal and modern dance groups like the Paul Taylor Dance Company and Pilobolus. I've often said that the most impressive athletes I've ever worked with were dancers. Their combination of strength and grace is unparalleled. It is hard to describe the beauty and power that they combine.

Imagine standing on one leg. Now, extend the knee of the other leg in the air.

Now, spread your arms out to the side. Now, raise up on your toes. Now, make it beautiful. And, of course, this is the simplest of their movements.

At times, it's as if they are levitating, motionless in the air for what seems like minutes. Chesterton eloquently describes a "perfect force," an "airiness that can maintain itself in the air."

Like the sun rising or setting on the ocean horizon, it is hard to describe to someone who has not experienced it. I was often backstage and at the location hours before the performances. I watched their orchestrated processes from preparation to performance onstage. I marveled at their ability to perform precision and beauty, with movements of leaping and holding positions, their bodies, and their partners, night after night, knowing that the three or four shows that they were doing in our city were only part of a twenty- or thirty-city tour.

What is the formula for this combination of strength, control, and endurance? Dancing athletes are serious students of many of the resiliency principles we have covered. They deliberately practice sensory motor awareness and are masters of knowing where they stand and how their bodies move. They must have a keen sense of where they are.

Chesterton again, from his book *Orthodoxy*: "A bird is active, because a bird is soft. A stone is helpless, because a stone is hard. The stone must by its own nature go downwards, because hardness is weakness. The bird can of its nature go upwards, because fragility is force."

A bird, by its nature, can go upward. No other animal can do this. A Blackbird jet flying nearly two thousand miles per hour covers thirty-two of its own body lengths per second, but a common pigeon covers seventy-five of its body lengths per second. The roll rate of the aerobatic A-4 Skyhawk plane is about 720 degrees per second, while the roll rate of a barn swallow is more than 5,000 degrees per second. Some military aircraft can withstand gravitational forces of 8G–10G (Earth's gravity is equal to 1G). Many birds routinely experience g-forces greater than 10G and up to 14G. Maybe dancers are so impressive because they mimic and sustain the extraordinary performance qualities of birds better than anyone else!

Most of us can perceive and expect that dancers are masters of *letting go*. Their movements and expressions are so free and under control. What most do not see or appreciate are their processes of rest and creating space. Behind the curtain, they have specific methods that align with Jaku and Rubin's recommendations. I often saw them simply relaxing in unique postures for long periods, sometimes for improving mobility and just as often for simply mobilizing the mind. I would see them reading and having fun playing and socially engaging. Most fascinating was that all of this relaxation, more often than not, led right up to their demanding and exquisite performances.

Therefore, it seems clear that they applied activities of rest and relaxation similar to Jaku's lying down. Because they had prepared thousands of hours of deliberate practice and deep work, they could engage the demanding and powerful performances with precision. Eloquent execution, night after night.

What is likely less clear for these amazing dancing athletes and Jaku is how these difficult and stressful feats improved their resiliency and tolerance. Challenging activities, when pursued fearlessly, actually created more space and tolerance for stress. Such events and their experiences created space for improved resiliency to stress and, importantly, improved resiliency to unexpected stresses.

Therefore, while rest and sometimes leisure are valuable for creating space, it is likely that similar space creation and resiliency can happen through challenging activities. Preparation and poise in those challenging activities are important factors for success—priceless, really.

Masterly pursuit of your purpose(s) likely includes unique combinations of lying down and taking on challenging performances that are distinct and different for each of us. What parameters do you need to develop your *perfect force*?

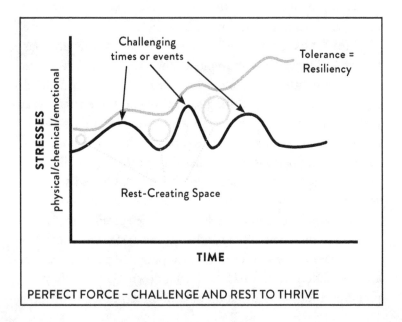

PERFECT FORCE – CHALLENGE AND REST TO THRIVE

TRAINING

LETTING GO PHYSICALLY AND MENTALLY

"Never give a sword to a man who can't dance."

Confucius

BREATHING

Breathing is important. We have been saying this for twenty-five years. Almost everyone is saying it now. Of course this isn't anything new under the sun. Most forms of attention to breathing are beneficial. Our recommendation is targeted toward improving the control of respiration in a way that also improves trunk and spinal stability. This approach to breathing improves the activation of the diaphragm, lower abdominal muscles, lateral trunk, and pelvic floor. When accomplished, this also reduces the activation or tightness of upper and lower back muscles as well as muscles of the hips, arms, and legs.

Lie on your back with your legs positioned on a box, ottoman, or small chair. This is usually the best and most neutral position, and your legs can completely relax. Be sure to have a medium-size pillow under your head. Place one hand on your chest and the other on your belly. Inhale through your nose and out through your mouth. Purse your lips like you're attempting to whistle. Do your best to have only your lower hand move during both inhalation and exhalation. Complete three to four breaths and then relax for approximately one minute. Repeat 6–8 times for a full period of approximately 15–20 minutes. Should you have any trouble during this exercise, consult your circle of advisors or a health practitioner.

WARNING—possible side effects include:

- *More relaxation*
- *More focus*
- *Feeling of meditation*
- *Less pain*

www.powerofdoingwhatmatters.com/videos

DO SOMETHING HARD—VOLUNTARILY

Throughout the book I have referenced that doing something hard is a value. This something can fall under physical or mental challenges. When deciding on a hard challenge, it is important to use your team to determine if you are fit for this particular challenge. Examples of hard challenges are: doing an escalating combination of push-ups, curl ups, and squats over a three-week interval; climbing a mountain; or staying on your feet for eighteen to twenty-four hours. It also could be a relatively simple task but something that's done consistently: taking a cold shower for twenty days, learning to juggle for twenty days, or doing your breathing exercises for a month. Success with these hard challenges requires commitment and accountability. An example of an agreement you make with yourself could be: "I will do this morning and night. If I miss a session, I have to start over."

> "A ship in the harbor is safe, but that is not what ships are built for."
>
> John A. Shedd

LIFT WEIGHTS

We were meant to lift, pull, and push. Our nervous system responds to these stresses.

Do some form of resistance exercise at least three times a week if you want to improve. Two times or less if you simply want to maintain. I would recommend checking with your circle of advisors on where you stand to lift, push, and pull weight. In addition to providing good stimuli to the nervous system, resistance training promotes lean muscle development and strength for being active, positioning you to do things that are hard and joyous.

Grip and lean muscle mass are the two factors most reliably linked to living longer and robustly.

Moving objects against resistance will improve both grip and muscle scores.

BE CHILDLIKE

For most of us, when we were three to five years old, we moved with less thought and fear and, therefore, moved better and more freely. As a result, our nervous system would find the best way possible to get the job done for whatever it was we were trying to do. Our joy would often burst through spontaneously during these movements. Remember Roger Bannister's story of how his joy of running on the beach stayed with him all his life? Explore and discover childlike activities that help to resurface your movement coordination and your exhilaration at getting to be on the playground. Roll in the grass, sprint, wrestle with your grandchildren, color, walk through the woods, jump or dive into the water, roll down a hill, ride a bicycle. Importantly, do it unabashedly, freely. Of course, do it often.

If you are not fit to do some of these activities, imagine the activity and move the parts you can. Watch children, toddlers, and infants. Let their eyes speak to you and move you. Both of my grandchildren had the habit of spontaneously asking me, "Are you happy, Papa?"

After receiving the tender, emotional punch to the nose, I would say, "Yeah, I'm happy."

Why wouldn't I be?

PART V

ACCESSING AND SUSTAINING POSITIVE RESPONSIVENESS

"Happiness is continuing to desire what one already has."

Saint Augustine of Hippo

WHERE YOU STAND

One of my early experiences with a professional athlete was a cornerstone moment for CIHP and what we understand about pain and performance today. The experience was important because of what we learned. He was a professional running back in the NFL. He weighed 240 pounds and was six feet, two inches tall. In the early 2000s, this was a tall and big running back. He was an amazing athlete. Think Hercules, the movie *300*, or your favorite superhero. He could run a forty-yard dash in 4.3 seconds. This is fast. Some of the fastest track and field sprinters of all time run the hundred-yard dash in ten seconds. He had this type of speed at this size! He was highly regarded because, at that size and that speed, he could run right over and through opposing players.

When I evaluated him, I discovered something fascinating. He had trouble standing on one leg. Remember, when we walk or run, we are on one leg 85 percent of the time. When I asked him to do a simple split squat, standing and bending one knee to the ground as if to pick something up, he nearly fell over. Repeatedly.

This amazing athlete, who could run and perform in incredible ways, was having difficulty performing simple movements like standing on one leg. He had no neurological findings or abnormalities. He simply didn't know where he was standing. He was having only back stiffness when I first evaluated him, but as his career continued, he would limp in with significant back troubles.

Your nervous system is the first to know if there is stress in your body. It is often months to years before symptoms appear or results show up on tests such as labs and imaging. We have all likely had the experience of a parent, spouse, friend, or colleague identifying that something is wrong with us before we tell them. This is your body's representation of what is stressing you and how you are handling it coming forward. That person sees it because they know you so well. They are familiar with your normal representation and see the difference. Grandparents are particularly good at this. They have developed a keen sense, and their lives have slowed down enough to see, hear, and feel more clearly.

One of my most influential teachers, mentors, and friends, Karel Lewit, said, "Feel the needs of your patients." Lewit, a professor of neurology at Charles University in Prague, was a master of listening to a patient's story. He taught that a good practitioner knows what is likely the problem with the patient before you touch them. He would say, "Your assessment should only confirm what you gathered from your history." The history in the clinical context is the conversation a practitioner has with his patient to understand their problem. Lewit was also gifted in the art of palpation. His ability to palpate a muscle or body part and know if there was a problem was extraordinary. He would repeatedly identify stress in the body far from the area of pain and routinely resolve the patient's condition without working on the area of pain. Lewit said, "The human hand is the greatest therapeutic tool that has been and ever will be invented."

Vladimir Janda, who was also a professor of neurology at Charles University in Prague, mentor, and friend, said, "Posture is the starting point for all movement." Janda would often watch someone walk across the room and diagnose them without knowing them or even having a conversation. The practitioners and therapists at Charles University were masters in seeing, hearing, and feeling the needs of the patient. They were passionate about knowing where a patient stood. Maybe they developed their expertise because they didn't have the advanced technical means as did more industrialized countries. Or perhaps, they developed these skills because they sensed it was best.

Early in my career I was blessed to be in their path and to learn and study with many of them. As technology has evolved, it is ironic that their mastery of seeing, hearing, and feeling the patient's needs is often the missing factor in a growing desire for resolving pain and building resiliency for most people today. Abraham Verghese, a respected physician and author, described over several interviews and publications how the current approach to healthcare has underestimated the value of human touch. He said, "Today's healthcare puts the majority of the attention to the patient in the computer and little to the patient in the bed."

There is a scene from the movie *The Big Short* where Jared Vennett (Ryan Gosling) is telling Mark Baum's (Steve Carell) group that the housing market is going to crash. I have played this clip countless times as it speaks to and runs parallel with what has been happening within our healthcare system over the last few decades.

Baum's group is baffled and cannot believe that all the banks, governments, and advisors would not see this coming. All these smart and well-meaning people. Vennett says, "No one is paying attention because the banks are too busy getting paid obscene fees." Of course, it did happen.

Verghese and many others have been suggesting a similar scenario with our healthcare system. What is sad is that he and others have been saying this for close to a decade. Part of the curious gap is that many of the suppliers, doctors, and hospitals feel the same way Verghese does. They are caring and know caring is important. Verghese says, "But we are prisoners of the healthcare systems . . . all gobbling from the same rich, multi-trillion-dollar trough."

Despite the fact that healthcare in the United States is

now approaching 20 percent of the US GDP, there are growing signs that people are beginning to pay attention. When you take steps to build your resiliency, you help shine the light on what Lewit, Janda, and Verghese have championed. Caring for patients is a human-to-human interaction. Imagine the changes that could occur if public demand shifted to the quality of care versus expediency. I think next steps, good things, are just around the bend.

At our institute, the work of Lewit, Janda, and others from the Prague school is foundational to our approach. One of the ways we are reflecting their skills of observation and interpretation is with our Visual Health Representations (VHR™). The VHR™ is a series of four standardized photographic images that are qualitatively and quantitatively scored. Your VHR™ reflects how your body is handling current and past stresses. Your body reacts to pain, injury, inflammation, poor movement, and fear. Your body also reacts to you being anxious, excited, joyful, sad, angry, and happy. All these reactions and responses are reflected outwardly and are represented in every one of us. It is what your grandparents and loved ones see. This information, which we gather from the VHR™, helps our doctors and therapists plan for diet, exercise, treatment, and other stress-reducing strategies. Maybe most importantly, to know if the plan is working or not.

CIHP has been using versions of VHR™ since its inception in 2003. After more than twenty thousand subjects, I am fascinated day after day by what we learn by taking the time to look at what the individual's body is expressing. Importantly, the VHR™ increases the value and attention to examining the patient or client. There are many ways to assess someone's health representation. The best practices will require looking, listening, and feeling. The most meaningful and productive ones will require time and a human. Who wouldn't like to know where they stand?

We were fortunate to work with the aforementioned football player for many years. During that time and after, he became one of the best running backs in the NFL. He became very good at standing on one leg, doing split squats, and knowing where he stands.

SWING

How do you know where you stand? Are you fit for resiliency?

The story of the University of Washington rowing team's amazing victory at the Berlin Olympic Games is most known through the bestselling book by Daniel Brown *The Boys in the Boat*.

Their accomplishment is legendary. It required physical, mental, and emotional preparation and performance. Week by week, day by day, moment by moment, they had to know where they stood. Their circle, coaches, trainers, and rowing team helped them know where they stood and what they needed to do. Physically, mentally, and emotionally.

The ultimate pursuit for eight-person rowing was called "swing."

Swing is the term used for the synchrony that is accomplished in eight-person rowing. George Pocock, the legendary boat builder and coach, also part of the team of the 1936 University of Washington rowing team, is often quoted for his eloquent descriptions of the harmony and rhythm involved in achieving swing. He would reference how when achieved it was seemingly effortless. Pocock would often praise swing's beauty and that it was the closest thing to the divine. He would say, "Eight hearts have to beat as one . . . It is a pleasure to be in."

Swing can be accomplished when two or more individuals are working together and toward a common goal. The coordination, balance, and flow only reach magical moments of excellence and periods of extraordinary accomplishment when two or more have similar knowledge and experience. In other words, if you put four experienced rowers in the boat with four inexperienced rowers, it would be a long time before you would likely experience anything close to swing. Therefore, shared knowledge and experience is a necessary ingredient for swing. Pursuing something hard seems to make accomplishing swing more recognizable and enjoyable. The greater the number of individuals attempting swing, the harder it is. And like in eight-man rowing, when larger groups swing, it generates moments that are both incomprehensible and like coming home.

What if you pursue swing in all that you do? Many hearts attempting to beat as one. Like eight-man rowing, there must be similar knowledge and experience, and those involved must keep their mind in the boat. To keep your mind in the boat, you must trust others to do what is necessary for their role.

If you work toward creating swing with your team, you will have more moments of swing in your life. When you want it. When you need it.

Swing. It's a pleasure to be in.

BOAT

Winning the gold medal at the Berlin Olympics was the climax of the *Boys in the Boat* story. Each of the rowers, and maybe especially Joe Rantz, who was the main character in the book, would tell you there was a lifetime of journey still to go after that race.

One of my favorite parts of the book has to do with its creation. Daniel Brown describes meeting Rantz and interviewing him about the story of the 1936 University of Washington team. After their initial meeting, Rantz, who was then in his eighties, told Brown, "I am happy to share my story and have it written. As long as it is about the boat."

At this point in his life, and maybe sooner, Rantz seemed

to have a clear understanding of what was important to him. The joy and triumph during the race in Berlin, and the learning and successes that followed, were not due to him and maybe not even his team or coaches. It was about what happened in the boat. His story reflects a remarkable message of how preparation can come in many desirable and undesirable forms. How innate, immeasurable focus is best when shared between individuals and especially a team (swing). What is not covered is how to sustain, use, or grow those experiences.

It seems every other day new technologies and theories are coming out about how to increase our longevity, to live happier and/or more successful lives. Looking across the team of 1936 and adding Rantz's message about the boat suggests concepts and thinking that are simpler, not more complex. Doing less, not more. Looking to others, not ourselves.

> Where do you want to be standing in ten, twenty, or forty years?
>
> Does your plan include exploration for preparation, focus, and sustaining? For identifying, creating, and rejoicing in your boats?

George Yeomans Pocock has been one of my favorite individuals to learn from in the past ten years. Some of our best teachers can be those we have never met. I have taken words of wisdom Pocock wrote about boats, rowing, and teams and attempted to translate them to similar meanings for the body, living, and teams. Thank you, George. These are metaphors for our lives and performances.

> *A body is a sensitive thing, a multi-trillion-celled being, and if it isn't let go free, it doesn't work for you.*

Living your life is an art, not a frantic scramble. It must be lived with head power as well as hand power. From the first move, all thoughts of things other than doing what matters *must be blocked out. Your thoughts must be directed to you and your own body, always positive, never negative.*

Where is the spiritual value of living? The losing of self entirely to the cooperative effort of the crew on your journey.

TIME IS ON OUR SIDE

When we sit down with potential new clients at the institute, we often review where the individual wants to be in ten or twenty years. We ask this because we believe your current state of health and performance is reflective of what you did the past ten to twenty years. Your health and fitness are representative of how you have invested your time and attention. With this information and our assessments, we then plan the best way for you to invest your time and attention moving forward. We've seen it play out again and again: what you do now reflects where you will be two, ten, and twenty years from now.

In a 2023 *Wall Street Journal* article, Joe Pinsker reviewed several recent authors who have identified this type of reframing of investing and awareness of time and found it to be of high value. The article relates what we know as self-evident truths: spending time with our children or grandparents is more valuable than working an additional two hours, reading a book is more valuable than scrolling social media, and taking a walk is more valuable than watching five hours of Netflix. And, while most of us know these things, a curious gap exists between what we know and what we do.

The article also identifies time as something we invest in, something we can control. We can control what we put our attention to. Because time is limited, it may be one of the few words that can be on our "important" as well as "things we can control" lists.

One of the most valuable elements that I feel the article relays is that of future pacing or looking ahead and reflection. To look ahead and examine what you would like your choices to be or wish they might be or wish they had been. This is sometimes part of our consultations and conversations at the institute: "You don't want to look back and wish you had not given your best for your health or performance." Or "Future pace one, five, ten, twenty years out. See, hear, and feel what that is like. Now, look to the next few months. What would you want to commit to based on that view?"

Have you and your team looked ahead to determine the decisions and actions needed to reach your next event in the desired way? Do you have a desired event? What specifically should be done now? Doing your breathing exercise every day, getting your treatment, completing your assessments to know where you stand, eating a colorful plate, focusing on your movement, and doing something hard are likely candidates for your time investment list. When we know what, where, and how to invest our time and we commit to it, then time is on our side.

YES, DEAR

My wife and I went to a small country church after visiting some friends. Before the liturgy, the priest announced he would be giving a fiftieth anniversary blessing to a couple seated in the front pew. I noticed there were two full rows of family joining them. At the end of the service, the couple came up in front of the congregation. The priest asked them, "If you could give a newlywed couple or someone about to get married advice, what would it be?" The husband answered immediately, so fast it was like he'd been prepped for the question, or his answer reflected his skill and mastery that had been honed for fifty years. The husband offered just two words: "Yes, dear." Of course, this received an immediate laugh from the group. The wife was also very quick and assured with her response. She said, "Commitment and communication."

I knew others who had been married fifty years, but on that day, I felt a different level of awe. Maybe it was the quaint country church and the humble crowd. Maybe it was that I was now thirty years into my own marriage. And maybe it was all of that combined with this wonderful, seemingly authentic message from this couple. Fifty years of commitment and communication deserves our respect and maybe attention. What have you committed to for fifty years? Are there individuals in your circle that have?

If we break down his answer, "Yes, dear," it eloquently sums up two important aspects of resiliency—as well as remarkably, simultaneously complementing her answer, "Commitment and communication."

First, by saying "Yes, dear," there is a forced pause in one's response that, importantly, slows the likelihood of potential reaction. Reactions are often loaded with past bias and opinion. In almost every instance, it's better to be a responder instead of a reactor. Think "first responder" versus "nuclear reactor." Reactions are often negative or perceived negatively by the receiving party: your spouse, friend, or colleague. By pausing, you trigger a subtle consideration of the other's perspective and allow space for your response to be more about empathy and support. If, by chance, your opinion is contrary to the request or comment, by starting with "Yes, dear," it will almost always be received better by the other person. Sometimes even amazingly better.

Other phrases could be used that inspire a similar feeling and pause: "I can see that."

"That's fair."

"I hear what you are saying."

However, I think there are things to consider in the simple magic of "Yes, dear." "Yes" goes straight to all the other person's neurotags (a neuroscience term used to describe triggers in the brain linked to our memories of emotions and events) that understand that this response is in agreement with their statement, that it is positive and good. "Dear" goes straight to those neurotags that are associated with love, endearment, and caring. Boom!

You are committed and communicating.

Maybe keeping "Yes" is a starter. Or "Spot on" or "Perfect" or "Indeed," and follow it with the person's name or "my friend" or "good man" or "superstar" or "good thinker."

Or maybe keep it simple: "Yes."

One of the most influential things we can *do* for our physical and mental health is to align our purpose with helping others. Helping others is at the top of the list in many studies and stories for predicting longevity, happiness, and success. Curiously, marriage, friends, and faith are also always in the top ten.

This simple, selective word strategy accomplishes pausing, gaining perspective, and, maybe most importantly, helping and caring for others.

CONGRUENCE

In 1965, the Harvard Test of Inflected Acquisition was designed to pinpoint which students in a Boston public elementary school were gifted and more likely to excel and acquire information faster.

The test identified approximately 20% of the children as special learners. The teachers were made aware of the results, while the students were kept in the dark. A year later, IQ tests confirmed that the 20% identified by the test as gifted learners had improved their IQ more than the other students. Many by as much as 100%!

What was most relevant, however, was that the Harvard test was fake. It was a bogus test. So why did those kids improve?

Daniel Coyle, author of *The Culture Code*, proposes it is because the teachers *believed* the students would learn better and created a culture where it happened. A culture where the students' perceived talent became a reality.

This is a fascinating study, and it mirrors the mind-body research that is nudging us forward to change how we approach health and performance. These incredible feats, like the Harvard student study, are often discredited, rationalized, and/or viewed as a mystery or miracle. If the formula to achieve greatness, happiness, healing, or recovery is to wholly believe you can and only do those things essential to that process, why don't more people do it?

As I related in the introduction, I often get asked this specific question by patients or clients, after they have had good outcomes with pain or improving performance: "Why don't more people do this?!"

Again, the answer is "It's hard. It's really hard."

What makes it happen at our institute and in other circumstances is in what the teachers provided. It requires a culture that supports it. You have to create a culture that supports greatness, happiness, and healing and deflects what doesn't.

Congruently.

The teachers created the culture where students who were not gifted learners became gifted learners. The students performed in this way because they concurrently *believed*, along with the teachers, that they had the capacity to do extraordinary things. They were not expecting anything else. The randomly selected students responded to the certainty and expectation. Like water turning to ice.

Does your self-efficacy for what you desire have this congruency? To achieve such congruency may, at times, like the story in the Perception chapter, require running to the roar.

TO THE MOON

First Man, a movie about the Apollo 11 mission and the first man to walk on the moon, is a favorite of mine. It's loaded with forward thinking and purposeful messages.

One earnest scene involves Neil Armstrong's interview to become an astronaut. One of the scientists asks Armstrong (played by Ryan Gosling) why he thinks space travel is important. Armstrong describes how he has flown high above the Earth's atmosphere and how small the Earth seems from way up there. He talks about how that changed his perspective.

Armstrong goes on to describe how he is unsure what space travel will reveal. He seems to be articulating that he doesn't think we should be pursuing space exploration just to say we went into space. He expands that what he hopes going into space will do is allow us to see things that maybe we should have seen a long time ago.

I love his metaphor on perspective, and if you substitute "health" or "resiliency" for "space," you can see the parallels.

Words like "discover" and "exploration" are most often associated with unknown areas of geography or environment. When, in fact, some of the most important areas to explore and discover are often right in front of us. Within us.

Using the right words can open our creative view to see and understand things that maybe we should have seen a long time ago.

Space (health) travel requires a balance of science, logic, and imagination. It requires a culture of excellence and resiliency across the team.

There is nothing quite like discovering something, whether it's something new or rediscovering something you had lost.

Recently a seventy-year-old woman came in for a consultation, complaining about a pain radiating from her hip down to her leg. She had already had low back surgery consisting of a fusion of several vertebrae and a total hip replacement. After our assessments and the client viewing her images, she said, "Oh my, I'm standing on only one leg."

She was putting all her weight on one leg and, importantly, putting all her weight on the leg that was causing her pain.

Our recommendations were that she do three new stabilization exercises, including breathing and one-leg standing, and do nothing else. No more yoga, stretching, or other exercises. To be clear, yoga and stretching are not undesirable by themselves. They were simply not good for this client at this time. Three weeks later, we conducted new assessments including VHR™ and body composition measures. She had complied diligently, doing the exercises that we had recommended and nothing else.

Knowing the results of her reassessments, I asked, "How are you doing?"

She replied, "Well, a little better. I still have pain; however, some movement is better and stronger."

We then reviewed her new assessments. Her VHR™ had changed dramatically! There were no longer sagging tissues in her abdomen, and there was new tone in her torso. Her overall posture was very improved. She was no longer standing on her painful leg.

I then asked her if she had changed her diet during those three weeks.

She emphatically replied, "Oh no, not at all. It was during the holidays."

"Well," I said, "the reason I ask is that in addition to these visual changes on your images, you've gained three pounds of lean muscle and lost two percent body fat!"

She had done less physical activity, and she had gained

muscle and lost fat. She had not changed her diet. Because she had performed movements that hit the neurological target and did not do movements that missed, she won. She hit the portal in the Death Star.

Most notable, and fascinating, was that after these observations and discussion, our client said, "You know, I actually am feeling a lot better." Phase transition.

Sometimes answers to our questions are right in front of us. Things we should have seen a long time ago but just hadn't been able to until now.

Here's to steady and persistent exploration.

KIND OF NEAT

From the same movie and the same scene, Armstrong (Gosling) has nearly finished his interview, and all the astronauts around the table are smiling and posturing their thumbs up for Armstrong as a good candidate, when one of the administrators decides to ask one more question. He inquires about Neil's daughter's recent death due to brain cancer. Neil stoically acknowledges that his daughter did die of brain cancer, and he looks for another question. The other interviewers in the room are ready to move on, but the same administrator inquires one more time. Sheepishly, he asks if Neil thinks this will have an effect.

Armstrong, after a pause, says, "Well, I think it would be unreasonable to think it wouldn't have an effect."

In our previous chapters we have touched on how complex and unbelievable our bodies and minds are. We discussed how there are trillions of cellular interactions happening every moment, and we reviewed how there are more cellular interactions in one occurrence of pain than there are stars. Through the examples of Prefontaine, Barty, and Kipchoge, we have shown how the human body, and particularly the nervous system, can adapt and do miraculous things. It would be unreasonable to think that these and all the potential cellular interactions that occur during each moment, like Armstrong's experience with his daughter, would not have an effect.

Not a day goes by in our client consulting and training that we are not attending to similar conceptions of reasoning. Individuals trying to recover from pain, regain their physical fitness, recover from surgery, or improve and excel in their craft or sport, whether professional or amateur.

The dialogue often surfaces around these areas of discovery. I might ask them, "How long do you think you have been moving like this or experiencing these pain episodes?" or "How long do you think it has taken you to get into this situation?"

Most will answer sincerely and humbly, "Ten years," "Twenty years," or at least "Several years."

And then I will add, "Do you think over this time period you have developed physical and emotional patterns related to these situations?"

They say emphatically, "Absolutely." "It has made my life miserable." "I can't do anything I love doing." "I cannot perform as consistently as I know I can."

Thus, if we can appreciate the complexity of trillions of cells patterning and developing our physical, mental, and emotional states, then can we imagine what's involved in ten years of low back pain, surgery for our knee, chronic digestive disorder, chronic inflammation, poor putting on the golf course . . . twenty years of relationships . . . ? Is it reasonable to think that we are going to be able to change something in a sustainable way in a few days? A week, months?

When I say "sustainable way," it's an important qualification. On our treatment table we can often improve or resolve someone's pain within one session. A medication or surgery can often alleviate pain and/or many symptom presentations. We can often improve our putting stroke several times during a practice session. In fact, with most athletic performances, during practice sessions or second attempts, we are very successful. But, to sustain these effects almost always requires a thorough understanding of all the representations that are currently in place (Perception). It requires deliberate practice of *doing what matters* to create a new representation that affords the changes desired (Persistence). The practice usually takes a reasonable amount of time that is relative to the time the previous undesirable representation has existed (Patience).

We lean toward this illogical expectation of a quick fix because we have been encouraged to do so. Our culture, medical and otherwise, has shifted our thinking to expect the illogical. To want and desire comfort and resolution without consideration of the history and background involved. Immediate gratification at any cost. We are conditioned to pursue "one thing" that is linked to our problems and, therefore, "one thing" that will solve our problems. Your low back pain is due to a degenerative disc, and therefore, if you take this medicine, have this surgery, or even do this exercise, it will resolve it.

Logically, psychoneuroimmunologically, our problems or conditions or desires for performance are rarely, if ever, due to "one thing." Therefore, they will not be resolved by "one thing."

Unfortunately, when we falsely pursue "one thing" and fail, it adds to our recovery timeline, and our emotional and physical compensations increase and grow into bigger problems. The majority of the time when you think improving your game or your score has to do with your club or equipment, you not only do not improve your game or score, but rather you further disguise the real problem.

And, when we falsely pursue "one thing" and it improves our symptoms, condition, or performance, it moves our attention away from staying mindful about the other things that are important for sustaining mind-body health. Ellen Langer is a research psychologist, and with over two hundred published papers on mind-body therapy, she is sometimes called the "mother of mindfulness." One of my favorite quotes of hers is "When you think you know, you stop paying attention."

Related to our previous discussion, if you think you know that "one thing" is causing all your problems, you will likely stop exploring, discovering, and paying attention to anything else.

In another segment of *First Man*, Armstrong has just come home from one of his early days on the job of being an astronaut. Over dinner, his wife, played wonderfully by Claire Foy, asks how his day went.

Armstrong says, "Well, it was kind of neat." He then goes on to describe how the space module has to go through orbit around the Earth, and then how they have to figure out how to get the space module to reconnect with the spaceship without getting thrown into outer space. Armstrong concludes his review of the complicated and exciting scenario with "It's kind of neat."

Janet (Foy) responds with an enduring chuckle. "Huh, kind of neat?"

While they can be vast, complex, and sometimes mysterious, having an understanding of our bodies and minds is within our reach. Controlling our bodies would be an unreasonable expectation because that would entail controlling external environments and others. Expecting to control these things would lead to "squeezing the glass." Having an understanding of our bodies and minds is in our control. This requires deliberately pursuing knowledge and experiences to increase our domain and literacy about *our* current state. *Doing* our best to understand the trillions of interactions that got us here, at this moment. And what it will take to move us to *doing what matters* to get us where we want to go. Kind of neat.

PEARLS EVERY DAY

In small resilience group discussions, we review "Pearls Before Breakfast," the 2007 attention experiment conducted by the *Washington Post*. The article by the same name won a Pulitzer Prize. The *Washington Post* placed world-renowned violinist Joshua Bell at the top of an escalator in the subway system of Washington, DC. He played his two-hundred-year-old Stradivarius violin in a baseball cap. The experiment was to see if anyone would notice. How many would recognize that one of the greatest musicians in the world was only four feet from them, playing some of the most impactful music ever written?

The result: only 6 out of 1,075 people stopped to listen.

There was a fascinating subgroup of individuals that did notice Bell.

Three of the six individuals who stopped to listen had extensive violin-playing or music-studying history. One had seen Bell only three weeks earlier.

What is suggested about this group? For these individuals, recognizing that something great was in their midst was largely dependent on them knowing what this type of greatness was. Having familiarity. At some point in their life, they had chosen to focus on it. They had experienced it before.

The other subgroup recognized Bell's greatness but didn't stop to enjoy. They didn't stop to enjoy because their parents didn't let them. Yes, every child looked and tried to go see what was so extraordinary, yet their parents pulled them away.

Children's attention is open and eager for exploration. Children are less distracted by the less extraordinary and nonessential things and thoughts. We apparently mature into those.

In fact, some of the highest levels of artificial intelligence

(AI) in development are now being trained on babies in efforts to advance their work in understanding performance. Yes, elite military, Google, and others are studying infant and toddler behavior. Through observational experiments, child psychology researchers suggest that babies have an extraordinary, uninhibited, and unbiased exploratory capacity. Their social learning skills seem to comprehend intentions with few or no words. My three- and six-year-old grandchildren sometimes answer my questions before I am finished. Accurately and respectively. Their perspective, it seems, may be the one to model?

The first group that stopped to watch Bell—the individuals with a classical violin background—suggests that effort toward focusing on extraordinary things is likely to give us the best chance to see, hear, feel, smell, and taste extraordinary things. And, very importantly, to know the difference! Of course, this can be applied to performance or things we want or desire. And, on maybe a more basic, important level, things like love, beauty, and caring for others.

From the second group, the curious toddlers, we get yet another confirmation on perspective. This suggests that the most in-depth exploration and discovery occurs with open and untethered eyes, ears, and feelings. As is recommended in the training "Be Childlike," observe babies and toddlers. How they move and behave is something to pay attention to, marvel at, and practice! Move and live a better life through them.

Focusing on extraordinary things is likely to give us the best chance to see, hear, feel, smell, and taste extraordinary things and to know the difference!

KEEP EYE ON BALL

In the winter of 2020, during our meetings with CIHP team members in St. Louis, we covered things on our "important" and "control" lists. We spoke of Hashim Khan, who is often referred to as the greatest of all time in the game of squash, "the Babe Ruth of squash." Khan's most important message about the game was "Keep eye on ball." Simple. Singular. His abbreviated English seems to make this common phrase, for sport and life, really land.

We spoke of our team and how they had continued to "keep their eyes on ball." They were empowering human performance, albeit at a distance, through increased communication and cooperation. Our digital services were producing windows of magic and joy by joining staff and clients in a different way and at a time when social interaction was at a premium.

We spoke of our clients and how they had continued to "keep their eyes on ball." Maintaining their focus on those things that they had established as important for their health and performance: diet, exercise, preventive treatment, and resiliency thinking and habits.

We spoke of the current times and the uncertainty of the COVID-19 crisis. Vivid and accepted uncertainty surrounded us. However, there were plenty of things that we knew. We knew that constructive, individualized diet; targeted exercise; self-care; and forward thinking and habits improved immunity and ultimately longevity. All of these could be on our "control" list.

We spoke of Stamatis Moraitis. He was living in the United States when he was diagnosed with late-stage cancer. He denied treatment and retreated to his homeland on the Greek island of Ikaria. He adapted the lifestyle of the island's remote culture, eating well, exercising, socializing, being around family, and having daily purpose. To his and his doctor's surprise, he did not die. Moraitis, in fact, outlived his doctor. Most of us cannot escape to an island culture where watches are not worn and days start at 10:00 a.m. But we can nudge our own lives in a direction of self-awareness, self-knowledge, and self-efficacy. And when we do, we create new experiences that combine to facilitate transformations.

At the institute, we were always clear that we respected the seriousness of the COVID-19 virus and its consequences. What we were encouraging was that it might be in everyone's interest to put equal or more, much more, attention to those things we know can reduce stress and provide resilience for the unknowns that may come our way tomorrow, or ten to twenty years from now. To echo Hashim Khan, simply "Keep eye on ball."

FORTUNATUS

Fortunatus is a Latin word meaning happy, lucky, rich, blessed.

You may be familiar with Jesus's parable of the prodigal son.

While there are many lessons to pull from this story, the one that recently surfaced as something new to me was the perspective of the older son.

The younger son asks for his inheritance early, leaves home, lives wildly, spends it all, and becomes homeless. The older son continues to work hard, support his parents' interests, and live modestly. The younger son, after becoming homeless, comes back to seek refuge and support, and the father welcomes him with open arms, gives him gifts, and throws a party!

What the heck?

"What about me? I did everything right; I followed the rules and the moral path!" is the older son's reaction.

The father's answer to his older son's pride and anger is "My son, all I have is yours."

Here, maybe the father's "all" represents his land and riches. And maybe, it represents his forgiveness and gratitude.

The father is basically saying, "Are you serious? We are so fortunate!"

Consequently, forgiveness and gratitude are at the top of most lists of behaviors that predict happiness and reduce stress. It can be freeing. Doesn't it make sense to practice being more forgiving and grateful?

In 2019, Bianca Andreescu won the US Open tennis championship in New York. She was nineteen years old. She beat Serena Williams, a seasoned and world-renowned champion of the game, in the final match. Andreescu became the first

Canadian woman to win a major tennis title. Immediately after the match, she was interviewed in front of the fifty thousand people watching in the stands. When asked what this meant to her, she said, without tears and composed, "I am beyond grateful and truly blessed." She was direct and authentic. Her visual representation matched her words.

During times of such extreme emotion, what ultimately comes forward is usually what is at the surface. It is who you are. It would be very difficult to prepare to be grateful and blessed only when you win the US Open against the number-one player in the world.

During my coaching of elite performers, the initial desire or goal might be to be poised and relaxed in the batter's box or on the putting green. As soon as possible, we would try to change that pursuit to being a poised, relaxed person who from time to time would step into the batter's box or onto the putting green.

Filling yourself with who you want to be during those challenging times is the deliberate practice that will have those behaviors and responses at the surface when it matters. Having them there when it doesn't is the side effect.

I forgive you. I am grateful. Fill your heart and mind with these.

AIM HIGH. WOO-HOO!

I love the movie *A Charlie Brown Christmas*. I say "movie"; it's only thirty minutes. It's an incredible message that was produced in 1965! It may be even more relevant today. Someday I hope to write about the entire show. For now, I am surfacing one element of Linus's classic speech on the meaning of Christmas.

Most know of Linus's bond with his blanket. He has it with him all the time. It rarely leaves his hands or side. In this movie he uses it to throw a snowball, as a shepherd's hood, and to support a Christmas tree. It's his companion, sword, and shield.

In the iconic scene where Linus inspires Charlie Brown, Linus is standing on the stage with his blanket, telling the story of the birth of a king in a manger as the meaning of Christmas. In the middle of his message, Linus tosses his blanket down and says, "Fear not." He concludes that this event changed the world, picks up his blanket, and walks off the stage. He then calmly walks up to Charlie Brown and says, "That's what Christmas is all about, Charlie Brown."

Charles Schulz, through his Linus character, wonderfully symbolized a moment of tacit courage and joy. To toss away the most important thing, his blanket, because of the seriousness and certainty of something greater.

My granddaughter, six years old, removed her training wheels during our last visit. When we left, she was riding her bike, but was very cautious and unsteady. She would stop, get off the bike, and walk it up and down steep inclines and around corners. When we returned one month later, I was surprised to see she was careening down her driveway and through the grass. "Woo-hoo!" she cheered.

For Christmas, she received a new, bigger bike. The new bike created more weight and size to maneuver. Uncertainty and fear returned. She again was walking her bike down the driveway and needing assistance stopping and starting. I could tell she was focused and quickly gaining confidence and trust with each attempt. Her trust was growing like the Grinch's heart. We've all experienced this. On a bike, skiing, skating, or swimming. As you have success with your ability, your exhilaration to do more grows. In a short time, half a block, she was zooming along, her skirt and red hair whipping in the wind. Cruising up and down hills, cheering, "Woo-hoo!"

My granddaughter, too, seemed to show a tacit courage and joy. Tossing aside unknowns and fear because of the certainty of something greater.

Michelangelo is recognized as one of the most extraordinary artists the world has known. He is lesser known for his resiliency and, like Joe Rantz and others in our stories, it is his resiliency that likely made him great. It took him four years to complete the *David* and three years to complete the Sistine Chapel. During the sculpting of the *David*, his father banned him from their family for being a sculptor. Michelangelo accepted the painting of the Sistine Chapel despite being a sculptor and having never performed fresco painting and having no previous commissions for painting of any kind. Like many great achievers, and most of us, there were many obstacles in his path and times when it would have been reasonable and expected for him to quit. He is said to have remarked, "The greater danger for most of us lies not in setting our aim too high and falling short; but in setting our aim too low and achieving our mark."

Michelangelo exemplified a tacit courage and joy throughout his career, jeopardizing his family, health, and career because of his seriousness and faith in something greater.

As you look ahead to the next year, approach it with the next five, ten, twenty years in mind.

Trust and fear not. Fear not and trust. Do what you need to do to have tacit courage and joy for serious and greater things. Toss down your blanket. Aim high. Woo-hoo!

TRAINING

ACCESSING AND SUSTAINING POSITIVE RESPONSIVENESS

"Details matter, it's worth waiting to get it right."

Steve Jobs

ESTABLISH YOUR CIRCLE

Before setting out to do hard things, lift weights, or other good things, it will be important to identify where you stand physically, physiologically, and emotionally. It is important to be fit for your resiliency and for whatever it is you are attempting to achieve. It will be important to establish a circle of advisors that can help you see where you stand, what your specific weaknesses are, and what is feasible and reasonable for you to pursue. The number-one reason people stop exercising is that they get injured. The number-one reason they stop their nutrition plan is that they don't like it. So, be smart. Establish your circle of talented and conscientious practitioners and advisors. Make sure they are asking good questions, taking time with their approach, and making recommendations based on you as an individual versus just science or trends.

While there are many constants and standard activities and exercises that will help you, your best *do what matters program* will be one distinctively designed for you. Your circle can help you identify and create your best approach. One that has the best chance of hitting the target à la Goldilocks.

Importantly, a good circle will help your program evolve and change with your changes.

As Eliud Kipchoge said, "100% of me is nothing compared to 1% of my team."

DELIBERATE LEISURE

Carve out a portion of your day for strict leisure. This qualifies as something that does not pertain to your work, your pursuit of sport, or your career. If it is something that you can be disappointed by or challenged by the outcome, then it does not qualify as leisure. For example, playing a tennis game where you might be challenged by the fact that you don't play well, or if you lose the game, is not leisure. Going on a run where you are attempting to set a certain pace or meet a certain outcome is not leisure. Going for a walk with your spouse or playing on the floor with your children or grandchildren is leisure. Taking a short stroll in your yard, reading a novel, or taking a drive in the country is leisure. Going to a live performance. Singing, dancing, laughing. Sport performances are good, yet sometimes the meaning of these have lost their way. If you can watch, listen, and feel in a meaningful way, and not be attached to the outcome, then they, too, can be part of your leisure. Anything that makes your heart and soul rejoice. Remember there is a need to make space for creative ideas, innovative thinking, and good things to find their way to you. Such leisure provides space for joy, and joy is the intersection of love, logic, and courage.

I remember one spring we were renting a townhome on the intracoastal in southern Florida. I was writing on my computer and could see the boat dock just outside our window. After a little while, I looked out and noticed an older gentleman, probably in his sixties, beginning to do some work on his boat. As I watched him, I could not help but recognize the relaxed and slow pace at which he went about cleaning and sorting things out on his boat. He was clearly getting some work done, but there was no hurry or worry. You might even call it "piddling." This was close to fifteen years ago, and I still remember what an impression it made upon me. At that time and now, I realized that guy was adding years to his life. He was letting go and creating space.

Deliberate leisure needn't be a sport or lying on a hammock.

It can be cleaning up a boat or your yard. Feeling and smelling the dirt, seeing the blue sky and clouds, hearing the lapping of the water, feeling the wind on your face.

A client of mine was playing golf and was dialed in to doing what matters. He played with his wife and focused on the experience and sensations of being outdoors. The beauty of the course and rolling hills, the sounds of the birds, the wind and calm atmosphere. He focused on having fun and being thankful for his ability to play golf on a gorgeous day. He was creating space. He accessed information from his recent reading, breathing, and constructive words and thoughts. He also stopped some practice strategies that we had discussed were unnecessary. He stated he thoroughly enjoyed the day. A side effect was he shot the lowest round of his life. Whoops.

NEUROMUSCULOSKELETAL (NMS) HYGIENE

Every day, be sure to brush your brain. On your own, or with the assistance of your circle of advisors, identify and perform movements and exercises that make your nervous system come alive. The primary criteria for NMS hygiene are that it's thoughtful, slow, and follows basic neurodevelopmental patterns of movement. The breathing and one-leg stance exercises in the part II training section are examples of NMS hygiene. Most of us are very diligent and habituated to keeping the habits of washing our bodies and our face, and brushing or flossing our teeth. These are fairly established modes of hygiene that help fend off disease. NMS hygiene serves to provide regular stimulation and activation to our muscles, joints, and, most importantly, our nervous system. It seems more than logical that if we are going to be consistent with our hygiene for our body, we would do some form of hygiene for the system that controls everything that goes on in our body: our nervous system!

Some is better than none. On mornings when I have not ordered my time well and I have allowed some hurry into my space, I will still get some NMS hygiene completed. I do not walk out the door without getting on the floor or on the table and stimulating my nervous system.

It is a must versus a should.

PROWESS DEVELOPMENT

Make an attempt at gaining extraordinary prowess in at least one of your senses. Isn't it fascinating how most dogs love putting their head out of the window of a car going thirty miles per hour? Dogs, with their heightened sense of smell, are simply wanting more. They do the same with a simple walk in the yard. Exhilarated and engaged with their experience. Growing their prowess with each event.

When you move from a chair, or your bed, do it with precision of execution. When you toss a piece of paper in the trash, make it a skillful event. Build toward becoming a stealth walker. How quiet can you walk? Practice brushing your teeth with your opposite hand. Put your shirt, blouse, or coat on leading with the opposite hand that you are used to. Challenging these efforts of coordination will improve your sensory motor awareness. When you take your towel from the rack or hook, lift it intelligently, like a watchmaker, to minimize stress to the device. After hundreds of stressful pulls, the hook or rail becomes loose when you force it. The same happens to your body.

Take a walk in the rain. Without a raincoat. Barefoot is even better. At least for twenty minutes and alone. Notice how your visual and auditory senses come alive. I vividly remember on a three-day river trip when it rained nearly twenty-four seven. We were on the water and were being showered with water. The tents were wet. The food was wet. It was an amazing sensory experience. It was priceless.

In the past few years, I have also gone for a walk in fourteen inches of snow at -65°F and read for an hour in 125°F. Of course, be smart and safe in all these pursuits and endeavors. The more you explore the boundaries of your senses, the greater your prowess.

Listen to understand. See to discover. Feel to explore.

NEXT STEPS

"The more I understood about Christianity, the more I found that while it had established a rule and order, the chief aim of that order was to let good things run wild."

G. K. Chesterton

"Genuine education turns mirrors into windows."

Sydney J. Harris

"It takes courage to teach."

Karel Lewit

GOOD THINGS

Rebecca was the midwife for my daughter's first two pregnancies. She was this wonderful bundle of energy that shouted assurance and certainty. You could feel her authenticity. I loved her clever and deliberate ways of providing information and advice. An emergency room nurse in her first career, she would use stories and her experiences of over one thousand at-home births to help you understand. Rarely directing or declaring, she would say things like "Well, what I have found is you cannot speed up a delivery, but you sure can slow it down." I have found this also to be true with building resiliency, improving health, or recovering from pain. It is difficult to speed it up. But it is very easy to slow the process down.

Rebecca was brilliant at building self-efficacy for her new mothers. She taught other women, from across the country, the art and science of midwifery. And though Rebecca didn't know it, she taught me a lot. I was fascinated at how she invested her heart and soul into her practice. I once asked her what her purpose was. She said, without a moment's pause, "My purpose is God."

Then without hesitation, lingering, or boasting, she said, "I try to make the birthing experience as relaxed and stress-free as possible: for the baby, the mother, and the family. When the birth experience is positive, it positively impacts the child and the family's lives for many years to come."

Rebecca was a game changer for my daughter and our family's lives.

One of my favorite encounters with her was during a period when my daughter's second baby was crying incessantly and often without remedy. She calmly told my daughter, "There are probably fifty ways to get a baby to stop crying." What she appeared to be saying was it is sometimes a mystery why a baby is crying, and that things eventually sort themselves out. And that accepting this uncertainty as certainty was the shortest way home. Mystery is part of our daily existence and often essential for our resilience building. Acknowledging mystery is letting go. Thinking you can understand everything is constipating. Don't squeeze the glass. Hold on loosely. There are at least fifty ways, many ways, for you to build your resiliency for mental and physical health. There are likely some specific things that will get you there faster. Only you and your circle can determine what those best things are. If uncertain, focus on the known good things. Some are suggested in this book. As stated, be sure not to slow it down by doing undesirable things. Erring on doing less is usually best. Our repeated phrase to our clients from around the world is *"Do* these things on your list and nothing else." The "nothing else" is the hardest part.

As I write this, I am not declaring that I am an expert at *doing what matters*. I, more frequently than I like, find myself allowing physical and emotional distractions. Every now and then, even an undesirable word! If someone tells you they are an expert at *doing what matters*, be curious. Remember the elite performers described in the introduction? They don't think they are elite or certainly do not declare it. In fact, if you hear someone express pride in themselves *doing what matters* or claiming expertise, send them love and run the other way.

It is important to appreciate the math: $2 + -3 = -1$. To learn to change where you are today, you must end with a positive value in your equation of thoughts and actions. The confusion and failures often occur because we focus on past, current, or future negative thoughts or actions: *Don't eat this, don't do those exercises, don't think like that.* It is impossible to improve your equation and outcome when you place your attention on not doing or thinking about things you should not do. Instead, you will add to your losing. Unfortunately, you won't know until the game is over and your total score is in the red, you have overdrawn your account, or the negatives have accumulated into problems like pain, sadness, and disease.

More than likely, by the time you are reading this book, you have accumulated a net negative on thoughts and actions. Remember from our word training that there are three times as many negative to positive words in the English language. Additionally, and unfortunately, it is suggested that the influences of negative thoughts and actions carry significant weight. Therefore, it requires four positive thoughts and actions to balance one negative. Some of you may be in a better position than others. The most assured way to get back into positive numbers is to fill your days with good things. Good words, good people, good food, good thoughts, good movement, and more.

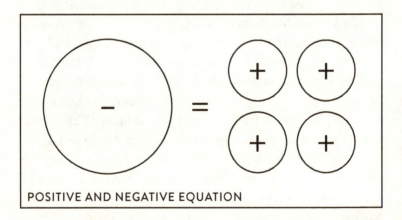

POSITIVE AND NEGATIVE EQUATION

This cannot be loosely applied. As we said in the beginning, it must be deliberate practice and deep work. Especially in the beginning. Especially when things seem hard. Especially for the rest of your life.

When we are looking for a new house, car, or clothes, we start seeing more of them! Were they there before? Fascinatingly, what we put our attention to increases our ability to see, hear, and feel those things. This is called the Baader-Meinhof effect. No matter the experience, we can really attend to either what is good or what is undesirable. It is one of the things we can control. Even if it is an experience repeated over and over, we can still attend to the bright spots and/or look for them. And when we do, our experience and learning will move us toward similar good things. Just like houses, cars, and clothes, we will start seeing more of the things we are attending to!

Being attentive to turning mirrors into windows can be very helpful. Keep your focus on others. When having an undesirable experience, do your best to see through it versus how it reflects on you. Look hard, really. Ask yourself what is fascinating in this experience. What could I learn from others' perspectives? Or simply, what can I learn?

Live by your instincts. Contemplate with your mind and heart. Use your circle to check them from time to time. Periodically take inventory of your circle of friends. Do the same for your circle of advisors. Some can be in both groups.

For these principles of resiliency to become who you are, it will require learning. Learning is a change in behavior evoked by experience. To continue your experience, be deliberate and dedicated to the training recommended. The training in each section of this book is certainly not the only training that is good. It can be the foundation that helps other forms of training catch fire and allow you to build a lifetime of good things. The training is designed to move you toward relentlessly avoiding hurry and worry. To perceive stress as challenge versus threat.

Hopefully you will find yourself reading this book or at least parts of this work several times and in different seasons of your life. Try reading aloud. Attempt to create as many opportunities for contemplation as possible, through thinking, writing, and sharing with others. Thomas Aquinas said, "It is greater to illuminate something rather than just shed light. Just as it is better to share what has been contemplated, than to merely contemplate." Sharing in this way becomes a form of teaching, and this is one of the highest levels of learning. Teaching can be where you achieve the rhythm of *doing what matters*. The teacher learns more than the student, provided they stay curious and on purpose to help others. It can be one-on-one or with a group. The physicist Richard Feynman said, "If you really want to master something, teach it." If you really want to master your resilience to life's stresses, teach it or be capable of teaching it.

In time, there will be resiliency programs to expand these concepts. I want you to *do what matters* and experience good things. I trust we can encourage others to do the same. When we *do what matters*, we can close the curious gap between where we are and where we want to be.

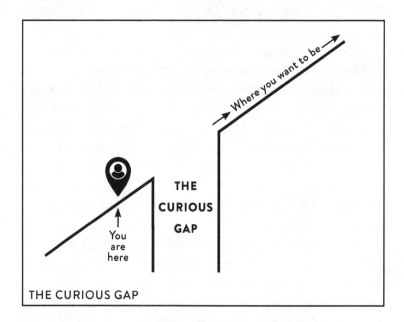

THE CURIOUS GAP

ACKNOWLEDGMENTS

I am grateful for the opportunity to share the journey of pain recovery, rehabilitation, and performance experiences with athletes and individuals in the many clinical and training environments across my thirty plus years of work. There is no encounter or learning without you.

I am grateful for the many small moments with friends, family, and teachers that helped put me on the path of caring for others, especially Tom, Kevin, Larry, Rusty, Mrs. O'Neal, and Dr. Kettner.

I am grateful to be put on the path of extraordinary teachers that shaped my thinking. I am especially thankful to Drs. Karel Lewit, Vladimar Janda, Stuart McGill, Pavol Kolar, Craig Liebenson, and Jerry Hyman.

To many teaching, clinical, and research colleagues who helped me learn to explore and write.

To my colleagues at CIHP and Dr. Jim George my partner of 20 years. I could not have helped others and filled this book without you.

For your succinct and valuable guidance on book development, thank you, Mark. Thank you, Jennifer, for your early critiques and support.

Thank you to everyone at GFP, especially Karen, Adria,

and Kylee. Sara, thank you for holding me to deadlines and making sure I love it.

I want to thank my parents and grandparents for teaching me early and steady lessons on love and family.

Thank you to my daughter and her wonderful family for their unending examples of courage, faith, and joy.

To my wife, for being there to inspire me from the beginning and helping me aspire to what really matters.

ABOUT THE AUTHOR

Clayton Skaggs, DC, is the founder and CEO of Central Institute for Human Performance and the founder of the Karel Lewit Clinic and Curious Gap Labs. In addition to his clinical career, Dr. Skaggs has been on doctoral, postdoctoral and research faculties of eight national and international universities. He has worked with thousands of elite athletes, military professionals, and executives. He consults individuals from around the world who have unresolved pain or injuries, or who desire better resilience.

Printed in the USA
CPSIA information can be obtained
at www.ICGtesting.com
CBHW020753081124
17080CB00019B/99/J